THE FREEDOM CHALLENGE

Mastering Emotions, Restoring Honour to Leadership

Brenda Oliver

Trafford PUBLISHING® www.trafford.com
North America & international
toll-free: 1 888 232 4444 (USA & Canada)
fax: 812 355 4082

CONTENTS

DEDICATION

This book is dedicated to my Children, Grandchildren and those that follow...

"I have walked that long road to freedom. I have tried not to falter; I have made missteps along the way. But I have discovered the secret that after climbing a great hill, one only finds that there are many more hills to climb. I have taken a moment here to rest, to steal a view of the glorious vista that surrounds me, to look back on the distance I have come. But I can only rest for a moment, for with freedom come responsibilities, and I dare not linger, for my long walk is not ended. [1]

---

[1]   Nelson Mandela

PREFACE

The Freedom Challenge – *Mastering Emotions, Restoring Honour to Leadership* is a motivational and inspirational book for people in leadership who want to escalate their personal performance and transform their lives, relationships and careers.

This book is meant to benefit people's understanding of whom they are now and who they could become, and in so doing, allow them to achieve their fullest potential.

Furthermore, it is intended to help people uncover their personal challenges, and in this manner, determine what may be holding them back from experiencing their own personal freedoms.

The Freedom Challenge blends expert opinion of world leaders, academics, psychologists, philosophers, scientists and spiritual leaders with real life and business experience and expertise – taking the reader on a journey of self-discovery and instruction. This journey is about achieving personal success and thus becoming happier, healthier and enjoying peace of mind.

The premise of The Freedom Challenge is that leaders are everywhere - anyone that is in a position of influence – in business, families, sports teams, community. And, it is about understanding the basic concept that leaders have been given a tremendous responsibility - the power to preserve or destroy.

Becoming aware of how much influence one has over others, or vice versa, and understanding the difference between resonant or dissonant leadership, and its impact, is ultimately the stepping stone to transformation.

Today, appropriate and effective communication can advance or terminate relationships, block or accelerate personal performance and negatively or positively impact employee and family engagement. People need to accept and be accountable for even their smallest gestures and understand the effect that their behaviors and actions have on others - both in the short term and in the long run.

Erasing any collateral damage that one may have caused others is their first obligation and their ongoing responsibility is to limit any negative impact in the future. And, by understanding the impact that others may have had on them, initiate their own recovery process and re-boot their journey.

Accepting and implementing progressive behaviours, honourable leadership principles and philosophies can actively transform one's life, career and relationships - critical to honourable leadership and developing new leaders.

However and perhaps more importantly, understanding what destructive behaviours —either one's own or the behaviour of others - may be blocking one's transformation is paramount. Initiating the necessary changes one must make is the next critical phase. Otherwise, people may never fully realize their aspirations and remain stuck in the dark.

Are people, today's leaders, commendably managing setbacks and challenges or leaving a path of destruction along the way? In either case, how is this effecting their workplaces and families? How are they coping? Are they living in a world of denial and blame? Are their expectations realistic? Are they making conscious choices and decisions?

Learning how to achieve best performance not only takes emotional intelligence but an understanding of how human beings are able to effectually and suitably respond to daily stressors. And, it helps to understand how human beings function and why they say and do regrettable things. Developing ones self-awareness, and in turn, one's self-management is the cornerstone to achieving long term success in life – both for careers and for relationships.

Are leaders making choices and decisions from a position of power or are they giving away their power? Gaining personal insight takes time and effort, it requires people to face their truth and reflect on what they could do differently – perhaps even consider their own contribution.

The information contained within this book suggests alternative ways of thinking – introducing one's mind to a domain of processes and possibilities – perhaps, even viewing evidence from a new perspective.

Sometimes, people just need to take a leap of faith.

Brenda Oliver

CREATING A BETTER FUTURE

What We Desire

While everyone is unique with unique lives, the reality is that we all share so much. We are in constant transition, at home and at work, making important choices daily. We want calmer presents and futures for ourselves and for those around us. We want to clarify what we want now and what we want next. We want the freedoms that arise when we are no longer controlled by stress, anxiety and fear. We want to live with energy, respect and honour. We want health, happiness and peace of mind.

"The shortest and surest way to live with honour in the world is to be in reality what we would appear to be." [2]

Therefore, we must constantly evolve, reflect and respond to the needs and views of others to create a better future - learning from each other and sharing our unique knowledge, life lessons and insights. After all, it is our obligation to pass on our personal and professional experience and expertise to a wider community of individuals and professionals seeking new knowledge.

These words are devoted to nurturing the individual - and the collective - voices of those who read them. It is an opportunity for the reader to validate their thoughts, emotions, values and

---

[2]   Socrates

1

choices. To discover alternative ways of thinking, understand the vast effect of their feelings and become the very thing that they hope to experience.

"Be the change that you wish to see in the world" [3]

It is my hope that all who read this book will grow into and refine their own leadership voice, and one day, share their voice with those that follow. This will be achieved with rewarding work, good relationships and lives that value honour.

The Inspiration

After leaving the business world, a friend of mine asked me to join her for a seminar. After listening to the keynote speaker, a renowned psychologist, I was particularly intrigued by the message and the idea of taking my personal performance to a new level. I decided that this subject matter was what I wanted to focus on. Ah yes, my life's work!

Expanding my frame of reference, from a business development perspective to a personal growth perspective, was a daunting change. After all, I spent a challenging twenty year career trying to be a no-nonsense business professional – expected of a woman then.

"Only those who dare to fail greatly can ever achieve greatly." [4]

Passionate about these new insights, I became a certified practitioner in Emotional Intelligence. One year later, I gave my first Keynote Address on this very subject and at the same hotel where I had first taken that seminar.

---

[3]   Gandhi
[4]   John F. Kennedy

At the same time, I developed and launched an online coaching & mentoring network for women, The Country Club: Distinctive Voices, Dynamic Women.™ The Vision: A global network of women positively impacting their own lives and their own worlds through personal and professional growth, together, making a difference - crowning this vision with a Keynote at the Global Women's International Networking Conference in Rome, Italy.

An online inspirational message – quotation - on honourable leadership practices was routinely delivered weekly to members in the network. This may not be as impressive in today's social media environment, nevertheless, along with the interactive website, it was a technical achievement in 2002.

From those early beginnings, this coaching and mentoring network evolved to where it is today – a Leadership Development Practice - providing clients with the competitive advantage to transform their personal, professional and business performance through custom keynotes, professional development workshops, executive coaching and business consulting services.

This apparent insignificant choice to attend a seminar with a friend initiated my learning journey, leading to my own practice and spending my time speaking, coaching and consulting - both nationally and internationally. It has been more than twelve years since the initial launch and with continued research and development - the writing of this book. The exploration and work continues: changing old ideas, experiencing new wisdoms, making my corner of the world a better place.

I am grateful for the gift of sharing my experience and expertise with others and the opportunities and freedoms that I have been given to carry on. When experience and expertise embrace an honourable leadership perspective then lives, careers and relationships evolve to the next level of performance, satisfaction and success.

Setting the Stage

What freedoms are people continually searching for? Better relationships, successful careers, profitable businesses, financial stability, better health - so that they can ultimately be happier and more successful - achieving a better sense of self-worth and fulfillment? These are typically the longings of most and the results we can expect when we change our focus from "being about me" and "fear-of-loss" decision making to "helping others" and "understanding challenges from the other person's perspective". Unfortunately, some people feel that they have "been there" and "done that" and are not open to new possibilities.

"The biggest obstacle in learning something new is the belief that you already know it" [5]

When we can understand what is driving our behaviors and effectively manage our own lives, we will have a positive impact on the worlds around us. Those worlds around us being our friends, family, colleagues and clients - those we come in contact with whether it is for a "reason, a season or a lifetime." [6]

Also, when we can face the reality of our circumstance and expend our energy on positively impacting others, we will no longer be ruled by fear. We will be elevated to new and exciting levels of leadership, effectiveness and performance. We will begin to experience new freedoms.

We cannot keep doing the same things over and over again, using the same tools or conducting ourselves as we have always done in the past and expect a different outcome. We

---

[5]   Zen Philosophy
[6]   Brian A. Chalker

cannot solve any problem from the same level of consciousness, activity or performance level where the difficulty originated. And, we cannot simply wish that things were different - a wish is just an empty thought.

When we can change our thinking from "measuring failures" to "measuring successes" and tie what "we love to do and do well", with our "purpose", we will remain motivated and we will advance through each small win.

Therefore, this work is presented from a coaching and motivational perspective and the first step to freedom begins within each of us.

DISCOVERING SELF

Relearning New Processes

We live in an accelerating ever changing world. To do well in this shifting environment we need to unlearn old habits, conditioning and traditions and relearn new habits, methods and techniques - to remain ahead of the game at home and at work and achieve our fullest potential - self-actualization.

Learning new processes offers us an opportunity to try something new — to begin a journey of self-discovery. To travel down this road we must first let go of our old ways of doing things and allow ourselves to be open to new possibilities and approaches.

However, change is difficult because people simply do not like change. Change is an emotional and uncomfortable process. Therefore, people are more inclined to stay with the devil they know than the devil they do not. This sounds like a pessimist way of thinking, does it not?

"A pessimist sees the difficulty in every opportunity; an optimist sees the opportunity in every difficulty." [7]

This non-changing attitude will not support one's personal or professional growth nor make way for any opportunity. This kind of attitude blocks one from recognizing encouragement,

---

[7] Winston s. Churchill

reaching their full potential and claiming an altered possibility.

While working in corporate business with consumers in the private and public sectors, I first encountered the client mentality of "we have always done it that way." People, who were accustomed to doing things only one way and unwilling to adapt or be flexible to new ideas, left me bewildered and curious.

"The conditioned mind is the source of all the problems of the world." [8]

Why is it that those in leadership positions, the decision makers, when a process improvement is acknowledged, significant savings are recognized and even when there is no one left in the organization that knows why they are doing things that way in the first place, are still reluctant to step up and initiate change?

Naturally, people are disinclined to change - they are fearful of the unknown. More damaging to their growth is their unwillingness to take risk - dreading some personal repercussion versus the idea and hope of a rewarding outcome.

"The most damaging phrase in any language is: It's always been done that way." [9]

Let's face it; people do not want to lose what they already have, their jobs and relationships, even when it is not ideal! Therefore, the predicament of doing the same things over and over again remains; without change there is no growth. And without growth, people are on the fast track to mediocrity.

While the future depends on many things, it mostly depends on oneself. If it is going to be, it begins with me.

---

[8]   Deepak Chopra
[9]   Grace Hopper

The Entrepreneurial Spirit

Why do some people risk failure? Why are some people determined to come out on top? Why can some people take an idea from a single thought to a new reality? Why are some people able to go from humble beginnings to ultimate success?

I do not know about being "born" for business as many entrepreneurs imply. What I do know is this. I have always felt strongly about being treated justly. I have always wanted a clear understanding of expectations and objectives. And, I have always known that no matter what the objection, it was only a matter of time until I made the sale. "No" was never an option!

At twelve years old I was a cashier at the local supermarket. Knowing that I wasn't being paid fairly, I wanted a raise in pay - equal pay for equal work! I suppose I had some determination even then. Before approaching the owner and simply asking for that raise, I sourced out and secured another job for more money - a calculated risk. I received the raise.

As a high school student, leveraging that cashier position, I won a television - a twelve inch black and white. The fund raiser: the highest number of canned nuts sold. For me, going door to door was a non-starter. Selling one can at a time, too much energy and too little reward! Consequently, convincing the owner to set up a display, I price matched the one's being sold – at a cost of a penny per can. Two hundred and fourty-four cases of twelve cans per case were sold. The nearest competitor sold two and one-half cases. I won the television, although, that television cost me nearly thirty dollars. While I have no idea of the retail value at the time, years later, I sold that television for fifty dollars!

That same methodology for process improvement was incorporated into my years in business. For example, going retail store to retail store to establish one new merchant was a dreadfully slow process, when a presentation to a head office could result in hundreds of new clients. No matter what the existing practice, there is always a process improvement waiting to happen. We can accomplish whatever we set our minds to!

"The entrepreneurial spirit is a gift that inspires others to become the best they can be."[10]

Leaving the corporate world and becoming a business owner gave me the opportunity to fully express myself and be me. The idea that one can choose their desired outcome by writing their own script and design a business around their own interest and skill set is both exciting and motivational. The ability to have control over ones work environment, to choose where and when one works, is liberating. And, while taking those first steps into the unknown may feel awkward or others may question your sanity, you will never know what you are capable of unless you try.

"Everything is always impossible before it works. That's what entrepreneurs are all about. Doing what people have told them is impossible." [11]

Being a finalist in the 2013 Business Woman Entrepreneur of the Year Awards was rewarding - an honour - and re-energizing. An overnight success – ten years in the making!

Personal Effectiveness

Before any enterprise can be undertaken, the first order of business demands an understanding of where we are at. Beginning with the premise that we want to increase the success of our lives, relationships and careers, we must first understand the place that we are starting from followed by

[10] Sarah Pierce
[11] R.H. Greene

where we want to go. To do this, old habits, conditioning and traditions need to change.

Therefore, we need to do whatever it takes to change - to wake up. The best way to wake up is to know who we are, where we are going and what the future could be. Consequently, the present reality is the starting point and the future is open to all possibilities. Having an open mind is essential to starting the process.

Progress is impossible without change, and those who cannot change their minds, cannot change anything." [12]

Most people are under the impression that personal effectiveness is about personal growth or self-improvement. In reality, it is much more. Personal effectiveness is about self-discovery, accepting reality and taking action.

Discovering more about ourselves, becoming aware of how we have done things in the past - personally or professionally - and understanding what our impact has been on others, the more open our minds are to this new world of change and possibility.

"The real act of discovery consists not in finding new lands but seeing with new eyes." [13]

People are the most effective in their pursuit to change when they are committed to learn, when they consistently practice new behaviours and when they can ask for and receive honest feedback. Their ability to change – their success - is relative to what they focus on, how much time they spend doing it, the process they put in place and their ability to hold themselves accountable.

---

[12]   George Bernard Shaw
[13]   Marcel Proust

Personal effectiveness infuses an experience with hope, empathy, compassion, authenticity and transparency - underpinning honourable leadership. These truly powerful people want others to be powerful too and that is how you will know that they are honourable. Regrettably, some people still focus on the faults of others believing that those people need to change. While that may be true, changing others is definitely outside of one's control.

"You reshape the world by reshaping yourself; the question is not how to change others, but how to change yourself." [14]

By evoking our personal effectiveness, transformation begins - bringing about more wisdom to our daily experiences and leading more fulfilling lives. Afterwards, the worlds around us will begin to change.

The Formative Years

School was not as challenging as I thought it was at the time. In retrospect, I didn't devote much time to studying, although, that was a mistake. It may have improved my average student status. I recall my physical education teacher saying to me, "what does your boyfriend see in you, he is so smart!" Interesting...

I am also reminded of comments others have shared with me about their own lives. Being told that they will never amount to anything or that they are lazy, irresponsible and so on! While it is difficult to turn off reactions to what people might say or think; one can learn to "not listen" to everything that they have been told. By doing this, others opinions will not have a long lasting effect! Just because others have opinions does not mean that their opinions are right. Opinions are only

---

[14] Linda Francis and Gary Zukav

opinions - not educated advice. Who is to say that they know more about your situation than you do?

"We can't always control what happens to us, but we can always control how we react to it." [15]

When I was in grade one, in a one room school with eight grades and each row of children was a different grade, we had one teacher for all. I recall that my first eight months were encouraging. As a matter of fact, my recollection is that I was brilliant! At home, I could read an entire list of words for which I earned one penny.

As progression would have it, we moved to a new town, a new house and a new school with only two months left in the school year. With the change of schools, I was significantly behind in the grade one curriculum, nearly failing my first year. This set the tone for Grade Two. My Grade Two teacher was a disciplinarian – she was both physically and emotionally abusive.

My Dad was also a teacher. In those days, they used a strap in school if things got out of hand with their students. He kept one at home. In addition to being a teacher by day, he was also in the insurance business working evenings and weekends. During the day, my mother managed the office. These were hard working and busy times!

At the age of fifteen, a new baby sister was added to the family dynamic. I now had three siblings. Never mind the "dismay" of my Mother having a baby when I was a teenager - I was now the built-in baby sitter. When not at school or working as a cashier, I was taking care of my sister. It didn't end there. Chores were listed for me to complete on Saturdays, a written list so that I was not ambushed with just one more thing to do.

---

[15]   Robert Urich

Making dinner in the evenings, during most weekdays while my parents worked in the office, was the norm.

My life was not all work, although, I do not recall feeling carefree or just being a kid without responsibility. I did go to school dances, movies and played an instrument in the school band - as long as I returned straight home once these activities had ended. While there were many rules for me being the eldest; being first helped break ground for my brother and sisters. You are welcome!

In addition to teaching Sunday school, singing in the church choir and taking piano lessons, my girlfriend and I were also Girl Guide Leaders. We "worked well together" was the response we received when we handed in a combined detailed answer to a two question pre-written exam. Pressed for time, she answered one question and I answered the other. We received top marks no questions asked! This could have easily ended differently.

Recently, I was contacted by a former child that had been in my Sunday school class when I was a teenager. He wanted me to know that I had been a positive influence on him during his childhood years. How did I do that? Apparently, I would always listen to him and laugh at his jokes. How fortunate for me to understand the importance of even the smallest gesture and realize the "unbelievable" difference it made to another human being.

I grew up in one of the larger homes in our small town. A custom built, three bedroom split level which included the insurance office on the first floor. Inside the home, it was a different scene than the outward appearance. My mother suffered from chronic back problems, and most likely, clinical depression. My father had angry outbursts and was physically abusive. Whatever the cause, managing emotions and frustration was not his strong suit.

One's emotional state can flood a person's thinking mind temporarily leaving them unable to access any logic and reason. All their perspectives are lost and they are temporarily irrational. When one loses control, it takes eighteen minutes to get their intellectual mind back – to access their logic, their education, their common sense. This is not the time to resolve issues, during this precarious time frame, because no-one is thinking straight. This is why taking a break and disengaging is an important strategy. As human beings, we get angry and that is acceptable. However, how we effectually manage through this anger can make all the difference.

My childhood was full of stress and anxiety, contributing to my chubby existence. I thought I was experiencing hunger and so I would eat. Of-course, then I would feel better. Stress and anxiety creates a whole myriad of chemical effects, the most insidious of which is a craving for fatty and sugary foods. The cycle continued - feel bad, eat something!

As soon as I graduated, I left home. My boyfriend and I packed our stuff, left notes for our parents and moved out west. His parents were in Europe and my Mother was in the hospital. I suppose, it was unexpected and extremely unusual to move that far away from home. However, we did not give it much thought – our new found freedom – how exhilarating. Still, upon getting the news, our Mothers immediately planned our wedding – a result of their traditions and conditioning.

My new husband's anger and frustration could also get the better of him. During the last couple of years of our marriage, I experienced his growing disapproval. I suspect his constant search for criticisms of me helped him justify his behaviour. At the same time, he wanted to sell our home and raise our family on a sailboat in the harbor. While I thought I was protecting our family life, it turned out to be outside of my control. At the time, I just didn't get it!

"Avoiding danger is no safer in the long run than outright exposure." [16]

We were married ten years. We had two beautiful children, aged two and five, when we separated. He moved in with his girlfriend, we divorced. I had no idea that my life was about to get exceedingly worse before it got better.

---

[16] Helen Keller

BECOMING EXTRAORDINARY

Who are The Leaders

We all know people who are or have been exceptional. These people provide a model of great leadership and a feeling of calmness when we are around them. We enjoy their company and they energize us.

"People may forget what you say but they will never forget how you made them feel." [17]

While we typically think of leaders as Presidents and CEO's - while they can be - they are not necessarily those at the top of an organization. Leaders are everywhere because leaders are you and me. They are everyday people in positions to influence others: parents, sisters, brothers, aunts, uncles, teachers, coaches, managers, supervisors, politicians, celebrities, editors, presidents, executive, and academics.

"Each one of us will be a leader at some time in our lives. Whether we lead a family, a group of friends, or a larger segment of society, each of us will act in ways to influence others." [18]

Leaders are role models and vice versa. Unfortunately, just because people are in positions of leadership does not mean that they are good leaders or role models. However, it does

---

[17] Maya Angelou
[18] Sandra Day O'Connor

mean that whatever they say or do someone will be listening, watching and taking their lead from them. There is no better example than children. We all witness how children will repeat what you say and what you do, particularly, if you think they are not paying attention or you believe that they are out of earshot. Yes, indeed, where did they hear that word?

"Setting an example is not the main means of influencing another, it is the only means."[19]

In business, new hires and graduates, those ready to take over in business and society, begin emulating their immediate supervisors - basing their behaviors on the culture and disciplines of those at the top. In families, children emulate their older siblings, parents and authority figures.

Consequently, all people have the potential to be exceptional leaders and the obligation to be honourable leaders. Honourable leaders are aware of the relationship between themselves and the people around them and are in tune with, in sync with or on the same wavelength with those people.

Exceptional People

Think about who the exceptional people are in your life: a teacher, parent, brother, sister, professor or supervisor? Most people would identify with people that include their friends and family. Typically, when we begin to reflect on what behaviours make some of our friends and family exceptional, we find ourselves thinking thoughts like, for example, they inspire me, they energize me, they listen to me and they make time for me. And, while we may also consider someone exceptional because they are well organized and exercise great time management skills, these abilities are rarely

---

[19] Albert Einstein

mentioned when considering exceptional people's qualities and characteristics – their "progressive behaviours".

There are also those figures from history, for example, Nelson Mandela, Mother Theresa, Mahatma Gandhi, Helen Keller, Fred Astaire, Walt Disney, Enrico Caruso, Winston Churchill and Henry Ford – ordinary people, with unexpected challenges, who became exceptional leaders. How did they distinguish themselves? What "progressive behaviours" made them exceptional?

Exceptional people have been in my corner when I needed help - the trust of a former employer who vouched for me when I needed a bank loan, the compassion of a dear friend who gave me her Christmas bonus to buy presents for my children when I was a single parent, the patience and generosity of a former colleague who provided me with consulting expertise without expectation and the empathy of the men and women who delivered business support to help launch the online global network.

"Most of us have been touched deeply by a few important people: people who because of their feelings for us and their actions have helped us to become who we are today."[20]

For example, there is a story of a man who gave away his running shoes and the socks that he was wearing to a homeless person - walking the rest of the way home barefoot in his work boots. This is more extraordinary when you realize that he owned only two pairs of shoes and gave one of them away - struggling himself to find work.

Exceptional men and women know their strengths and their weaknesses and employ effective strategies that leverage their strengths and compensate for their weaknesses. They hold themselves accountable for changing their own lives. They

---

[20] Annie McKee

have a desire to learn, be creative, gain perspective, share experience and follow their dreams.

"Progressive behaviors" - virtues and strengths - are the qualities & characteristics that have been associated with exceptional people. Consider which of the following progressive behaviours mirrors or best defines the exceptional people in your life? Would someone consider you an exceptional person? Which of the "progressive behaviours" best describe you?

Progressive Behaviours™

- Adaptable
- Appreciative
- Authentic
- Builds Self Confidence In Others
- Builds Self Esteem In Others
- Calm
- Caring
- Coach
- Communicator
- Compassionate
- Confident
- Considerate
- Courageous
- Develops Others
- Directive
- Empathetic
- Encouraging
- Enthusiastic
- Fair
- Flexible
- Gives Clear Feedback
- Gathers Sufficient Detail

- Genuine
- Gives Recognition
- Giving
- Good Listener
- Good Sense of Humor
- Helpful
- Honest
- Inspirational
- Kind
- Loyal
- Makes Others Feel Good
- Makes the Time
- Motivational
- Never Gives Up
- Non-Critical
- Non-Judgmental
- Non-Threatening
- Open
- Optimistic
- Passionate
- Patient
- Positive
- Provides Instruction
- Reasonable

- Remains in Control
- Respectful
- Rewards Performance
- Shares with Others
- Supportive
- Trusting

Most "progressive behaviours" of exceptional people have nothing to do with how smart they are or whether or not they have a post-secondary degree, doctorate, MBA, are academics or have any other specific designation. As a matter of fact, Harvard University spent twenty years conducting research to better understand how a Harvard Education could contribute to someone's future success. The research followed graduates in Business, Law and Medicine – so we know two things for sure - they were smart and they were well educated.

Harvard's findings concluded that although their education did contribute to a smaller degree, emotional style competencies were found to be two times more important in contributing to their future success than was everything else combined. And other research, among graduates of Harvard University, indicated that those with the highest IQ scores did not become overly successful as compared to those with a lower IQ. Additionally, researchers found that eighty-one Illinois high school class valedictorians, each with the highest school average and all achieving excellent grades in college, by their late twenties, they were just average as compared with that of their peers in the same professions. In other words, academic qualifications do not help us deal with emotions, frustration and the other setbacks and challenges of life.

Therefore, if IQ accounts for 20% of success in people with equal promise, education and opportunity, what accounts for the other 80%? The Harvard study found that childhood abilities such as being able to handle frustrations, manage emotions and get along well with other people made the most difference.

"The most important ingredient to the formula of success knows how to get along with people." [21]

When we make the time to reflect and be honest with ourselves, we can learn how mastering these childhood abilities could positively impact our lives, relationships and careers. And, this may very well shed some light on our friends, family and colleague's relationships, career choices and life challenges.

When people are honest in all things, not just in what they say and do, but whom they are; their words and actions line up with who they claim to be. People shouldn't have to worry about other people's hidden agendas.

The Preservation Years

Traversing the next few years as a single parent was bewildering to say the least. We met and drew up our separation agreement without lawyers, my ex-husband making all of the notes and being in charge. The terms of the agreement could not be disputed as they were in his handwriting. To my benefit, custody of the children was never an issue.

During times of separation and divorce, while people can experience amicable relationships, they can also end up on the receiving end of bullying, emotional and verbal abuse. All destructive behaviour affects a family's well-being.

Are you letting negative results from your past ruin tomorrow's happiness? There is no point in wasting your energy. When you forgive someone, it does not condone their actions, it simply frees you from being their eternal victim.

---

[21] Teddy Roosevelt

And, it isn't something that you do for someone else; it is something that you do for yourself.

"Forgiving what we cannot forget creates a new way to remember. We can change the memory of our past into the hope for our future." [22]

Other challenges included my personal credit. The car and the utilities were not in my name and I didn't have my own credit card. Don't ask! In time, I managed to get a five hundred dollar line of credit on a visa card thanks to an exceptional bank manager's trust and good will.

As well, because my ex-husband insisted women stay home with their children and I agreed to do that, I gave up what could have been a promising career in the airline industry. While I supplemented our income with home daycare, this was no longer an option as a new single parent. I needed to go back to work. Without working outside the home in five years - with two children - it wouldn't be easy. I leveraged my previous airline experience, finding commissioned sales work in the travel industry.

Working required a drive of thirty minutes each way and subsidized daycare. The car was not the best, the battery needed a bang with a hammer to make it start, which gas attendants were kind enough to accommodate. One day, when a tire went flat, I walked home with both kids - carrying a toddler. I did not have the money to fix or replace it. It was a couple of miles - tears streaming down my face all the way. Some days, I could not go to work because I did not have the five dollars to buy the gas required to get me there and back. The "not so" good old days!

Working in the travel industry and then in corporate sales led to a "cattle call" of over one hundred candidates for an Account

---

[22] Lewis Smedes

Executive position. It was overwhelming. How would they even consider me for this job? Nonetheless, off I went in my navy blue suit - nervous and scared. They hired me! Of-course, I told them everything they wanted to hear - even that I could manage national accounts and was available to travel across Canada. I must have been successful leveraging my previous, and very limited, airline and travel industry experience.

With no idea how I was going to accomplish the child care issue, when I needed to travel, never mind the actual business expectation itself, I accepted the position and thought that I was definitely over my head. However, I thought about it this way. I would be no worse off if I lost this job versus not having tried for it in the first place. It was definitely hard work but I survived – and with health benefits! Eventually, when I began working for an even larger organization, a company car no less!

Thank goodness for my parents, they stayed with the children when I had to travel on business – by then they were retired. My father has since passed away due to heart disease and my mother is enjoying her independence as a great-grandmother.

Work was difficult and I was tired. Every evening required me to ready the kids for bed, set the alarm for midnight, get up and write reports or figure out some other problem before morning - without the help of internet searches - and get the children ready for school in the morning. It was at this time, if I had some kind of decision to make or problem to solve, I focused on it before falling asleep, and generally speaking, I would have the answer by morning. The subconscious mind was an awesome personal discovery, or so I thought.

"The intellect has little to do on the road to discovery. There comes a leap in consciousness, call it intuition or what you will, and the solution comes to you and you don't know how or why." [23]

---

[23] Albert Einstein

However, there were also days when I did not have food to eat or actually forgot to eat, which was different from the days that I just wasn't hungry, hard to believe now! During that time, I remember receiving a large bag of groceries on my doorstep - people can be very compassionate and generous.

Being forced to move and sell the house, my ex-husband wanted his share, and with no prospects of where I or the children would live, our only option was a small townhouse and not in an ideal area. Out of the blue, it occurred to me to buy my own house. If the financial result would be the same, what judge would make me sell my home and move my children? Listen to your gut, your intuition, your conscious mind and then, most importantly, follow through.

This meant that I would have to make the offer to purchase my home unconditionally; there was already a conditional offer on the house. And one other minor detail, I was not making enough money, at the time, to qualify for a mortgage. However, if I was able to buy back my own house and in the end was not able to make the payments, I could still move out. Once again, I felt I could not be any worse off than the position I was currently in.

With perseverance and fearlessness, I wrote a letter to the bank manager on my employer's letterhead stating an inflated salary in order to qualify for the mortgage. I needed to, not only buy my house back, but buy out his net share. I met with my employer and explained my dilemma. He suggested that I write a letter and he would sign it. I said, "I did - here it is"! He was clear that this did not mean I was getting a ten thousand dollar raise. Thank goodness for humorous, supportive and flexible leaders.

Over time, learning to go in the direction of my fear, disciplining myself and having a positive attitude has served me well. While it was not the easiest road to travel, it has been worth the struggle. Misery will always be an option!

When it was time to sell that house, the real estate market had recovered, I netted a tidy sum!

"The only disability in life is a bad attitude." [24]

While I thought I was alone, I have been receiving guidance all along. Blessings can come through negative circumstances, and if we can keep a positive attitude, we will experience positive results. If our attitudes are negative, we may never make the journeys intended for us. All things are temporary and will not last forever; nothing stays the same, in good times or in bad.

---

[24] Scott Hamilton

THE BATTLES WE FIGHT

Who We Are

Understanding what activities, situations or individuals can energize us, or completely deplete our energy, is an important stage. Every person wants to feel reenergized and we are always trying to manipulate each other for energy - either aggressively or passively - according to Dr. Richard Boyatzis PHD. This aggressive and or passive behaviour creates one of four distinct behavioural types: an intimidator, an interrogator, an aloof or a poor me.

An intimidator behaviour type influences others to become a poor me. A poor me behaviour type influences others to become an intimidator. An aloof behavioural type influences others to become an interrogator. An interrogator behaviour type influences others to become aloof. Sounds confusing - does it not?

Interrogators continuously probe and ask questions trying to find something wrong with someone else and once they do - they begin to criticize. If this criticizing strategy works for them, then, the person on the receiving end is pulled into their drama. Anytime a person is pulled into someone else's drama, they are removed from the present moment. When one is removed from the present moment, they cannot think straight.

This criticism or blaming makes the person on the receiving end feel put down. Being put down destroys their self-esteem, their self-confidence and they become defensive and angry. Also, if they are unable to effectively manage their anger, arguments and conflict follow. This person on the receiving end of this criticism becomes self-conscious around the interrogator, trying even harder to not do anything wrong, anything that could lead to even more criticism. All future "perceived" interactions create even more personal anxiety. And, as if this is not enough, they begin judging themselves by what the interrogator "might" be thinking of them. They begin putting themselves down – negative self-talk. This interrogator has influenced an aloof behaviour type.

Likewise, parents, for example, can influence their children's behavioural type. As a parent if we are not there for our children, not living in the present or simply ignoring them - whether we lead very busy lives or careers, are preoccupied, suffering from depression, divorce or something else - children can be influenced to become an aloof behaviour type – emotionally distanced. However, because being aloof does not generally get their parents attention, children can grow up resorting to probing and prying - becoming an interrogator. These children are now focused on finding fault or something wrong with their parents or others.

As a side note, asking "genuine questions of concern" is different than probing and prying. And, while asking questions is the preferred method of a non-triggering conversation and a coaching tool to help guide people to find their own solutions - exercise caution - questions can cross-over to interrogation and subsequently to controlling behaviours.

Intimidators, on the other hand, threaten you with bodily harm. This is bullying behaviour. And, those on the receiving end of this behaviour think that being timid or shy will save them. This generally does not work because intimidators usually do not care about others or what is happening in others' lives. They are, by and large, insensitive and centered on themselves.

This kind of intimidation behaviour forces those on the receiving end to become passive and a poor me type. Poor me behaviour tries to appeal to the intimidators sense of forgiveness, kindness and sympathy. If this doesn't work, they try and make the intimidator feel guilty about the destruction that they are causing. If none of these actions work, then those being intimidated will endure until they are big enough, old enough or strong enough, to fight aggression with aggression. Then, they become the intimidator.

People are struggling at home and at work. They feel that they can no longer cope with the behaviour of others. They cannot understand why those people behave the way that they do. And sometimes, they do not understand why they, themselves, behave the way that they do. Therefore, this model may help to explain some of the events in our own lives. Also, this model tells us that people will go to whatever extremes they feel necessary to gain control within their family. After that, this strategy becomes their main way of controlling others or getting energy from others. The behaviour that they always repeat – their habits! The good news is that we can change our habits.

People in leadership positions need to hold themselves accountable for their habits and become aware of the effect their behaviour and actions have on others - especially in the heat of the emotional moment. Are leaders influencing confident, well-adjusted and productive members of society or creating unreliable, needy citizens?

"The way you see people is the way you treat them, and the way you treat them is what they become." [25]

On the other hand, when we can treat people the way we believe they could be, no matter what stage they are at now,

---

[25] Jon Wolfgang von Goethe

then, they are free to choose another path - a new possibility - and that is what they can become.

Treating others as you wish to be treated is the golden rule. Treating others how they wish to be treated is as important; putting others first is a remarkable motivational lever. However, be mindful, people are motivated by very different things - while some may love public recognition, another person may be embarrassed by being the center of attention. Honourable leaders recognize other people's needs in the moment and adapt accordingly.

Destructive Behaviour

Consider how many times we have experienced road rage or read it about it in the news. Unfortunately, there is not a day that goes by that there is not a news item in this regard. In fact, recent statistics revealed that over 1500 deaths are attributed to road rage annually! [26]

Recently, the local news reported that after a young man received a two hundred dollar fine, he worked himself into such a state that the next day he preceded to ram, not one, but five police cars. This ended in a car chase that created an estimated one hundred thousand dollars in damages and a collection of unnecessary charges that could land him in jail. Impulsive behaviour - anger - can alter a person's life as they know it, changing an unfortunate and somewhat insignificant incident into a life changing event.

"Whatever is begun in anger ends in shame?" [27]

When you are driving and someone cuts you off, are you one of those people who wants to follow that person home and give them a piece of your mind? Or, are you a person who

---

[26]   CBC News Report 2015
[27]   Benjamin Franklin

understands that these people most likely did not see you coming and certainly would not have tried to cut you off on purpose. Do you think that people actually wake up in the morning wondering who they can upset? The fact is that most people, who might be upsetting you, are likely not aware that their behavior is doing so.

Impulsive behaviour and other "transformational roadblocks" - shortcomings or weaknesses - are what makes people "difficult to get along with" and what can create a whole backlash of issues both for them and for the person on the receiving end. Unfortunately, difficult behaviour does not only affect that person and ruin their day; it also affects everyone around them.

Keep in mind, we can all experience and be the perpetrator of some of these "roadblock" behaviours on occasion. After all, we are still human beings. However, even occasional offences do not excuse "difficult to get along with" behavior. It is our personal responsibility to become aware of what emotions are causing us to behave in destructive ways and make the necessary adjustments.

"Self-awareness is a skill that 90% of top performing leaders possess." [28]

Unfortunately, there are many difficult people that simply behave this way most of the time. This is who they are, who they have become. What were their circumstances? Who were their parents? Where did they go to school? How did they live? Who was their role model – at home and at work?

Knowing our strengths and weaknesses, understanding what emotions are driving our thoughts and behaviours and recognizing how negative self-talk can impact our well-being and performance is vital to honourable leadership. Without

---

[28]   Talent Smart

this fundamental foundation, we cannot expect to manage ourselves or the emotional environment around us. Without self-awareness, we simply cannot successfully navigate and manage all of the many setbacks and challenges that we may experience in our lifetime.

However, dealing with difficult people simply means dealing with difficult behaviour. And most importantly, recognizing when our difficult behaviour is contributing to that other person's difficult behaviour! This is an important notion to think about - whose behaviour came first? Therefore, in order to not be cast as a difficult person yourself, be mindful of when your "progressive behaviours" become misplaced from time to time, when you switch from pleasant to be around to the person that is "difficult to get along with".

To the degree that we are able to change our habits - from reacting or overreacting - to responding in a new and different way, we will be able to alter who we are, experience a new possibility and become our best self. And in this way, we can and will influence change in others.

Consider the alternative outcome to our lives, careers and relationships when we are able to change our leadership stance.

- Changing from "always completing something the same way" to "adjusting one's style".

- Changing from "knowing everything" to "a readiness to learn".

- Changing from "believing what one person has to say is more important or interesting than what others have to say" to "an ability to consider another person's point of view and accept feedback".

- Changing from "refusing to change" to "a willingness to be flexible and adaptable".

- Changing from "always being right" to "not being critical or blaming others".

- Changing from "not interrupting others and focused on life revolving around themselves" to "being aware and sensitive about what others are saying and going through in their lives".

- Changing from "feeling that one does not have to explain themselves because they are the "boss" or the parent - my way or the highway thinking" to "listening to others and not being difficult to get along with".

- Changing from "it is a person's right to speak the truth" to "understanding the impact of their words and not hurting someone else in the process".

Do you know anyone like this? Do you work for someone like this? Do you live with someone like this?

Transformational Roadblocks ™

- Angry
- Argumentative
- Blaming
- Body Language-
  Crossed Arms
- Character Attack
- Competitive
- Complaining
- Condescending
- Contradictory
- Controlling
- Critical
- Defensive
- Devalues Others
- Discounts Others
- Disparaging
  Comments
- Disrespectful
- Dominating
- Does Not Listen
- Embarrasses Others
- Facial Expressions -
  Scowling, Rolling eyes
- Favoritism

- Forces Opinions
- Harassing
- Hounds Others
- Impulsive
- Indecisive
- Innuendoes
- Interrupts
- Invalidates Others
- Jokes-Diversity
- Judgmental
- Jumps to Conclusion
- Loses Control-Rage
- Negative Repetition
- No Consideration
- Non - Directive
- Non - Supportive
- Not Accept Others As Equal
- Opinionated
- Rejection of Others or Ideas
- Promotes Negative Perception
- Screams
- Secretive
- Shuts Others Out
- Silent
- Singles Others Out
- Solicits Negative Remarks
- Swears
- Threatens
- Trivializes Others or Accomplishments
- Uncommunicative
- Undermines Others
- Unjustified Comments or Opinions
- Unpredictable
- Unsolicited Advice to Others
- Withholding
- Yell

People, who try and function, using these roadblock behaviours, will likely alienate the persons they live with and those they work with. Yet, they remain bewildered. Why they were not considered for that promotion. Why they were let go when their company merged with another. Why they do not have many friends and supporters. Why their relationships are broken. Unfortunately, many people in this position have spent too much time putting others down rather than building them up.

"You can't hold a man or woman down without staying down with them." [29]

---

[29] Booker T. Washington

How is the perspective that you have of yourself different from other people's perspective of you? What impact are you having on others? Other people's perception of you is your reality. Unfortunately, your friends and family will only tell you what you want to hear and will not give you the feedback that could actually benefit you.

"One of the more important ways that people can develop is to receive ratings of their performance known as 360-degree feedback; widely used in leadership development programs." [30]

That is why 360 degree feedback is so important - it allows people to receive honest, confidential and anonymous feedback from the people they work with. It typically includes the employee's co-workers, manager, peers and direct reports. Receiving honest feedback about one's self can be difficult to find and even more difficult to hear. Honest feedback is a gift that helps people to understand what might be holding them back. Which self-perceptions are congruent with the perceptions of others and which are not - identifying those "transformational roadblocks" that are limiting their progress and success - the ones which they are still denying? Closing the self-perception gap is essential for change.

Collateral Damage

The collateral damage to those on the receiving end of "roadblock" behaviours makes people feel angry, threatened and frustrated. People begin to withdraw, feel anxious, and become defensive and resentful. And, if they too are unable to effectively manage their frustrations - arguments and conflict follow.

"No-one can think clearly when their fists are clenched." [31]

---

[30]   Centre for Creative Leadership
[31]   George Jean Nathan

When a person is hurt and humiliated by someone else's destructive behaviour, they become tired and have no energy. However, the most curious dilemma is that they are unaware of what is causing them to feel this way. Slowly, and over time, destructive behaviour creeps up on people creating an inability to recognize or even react to threats.

There is also a significant negative impact on one's performance. People find themselves unable to concentrate, reading that same page over and over again. They cannot pay attention no matter how hard they try. They feel the effects of tension and exhaustion getting worse. They find themselves making errors in judgment and cannot seem to do the simplest thing. This type of distraction removes people from the present. With this non-present existence - presenteeism – people disengage.

"Impaired alertness is one of the greatest potential dangers of life." [32]

Have you ever been going somewhere and suddenly you realize that you have arrived - you do not remember the actual drive? Are you living in the present or are you on autopilot - living a robotic existence? Are you moving from place to place, going to work, coming home, making dinner, helping with homework - going through the motions? One day, you may realize that you missed out! You never fully appreciated the gifts that you were given – the gifts that you ignored or took for granted.

We need to wake up, be present and focused on where we are. If we are at work, then we need to be fully engaged at work and when we are at home, we need to be fully focused on our family. Early on, it became a necessity and a practice for me to separate, compartmentalize and park those thoughts, emotions and feelings. If I was at work but started thinking of what I had to do at home with the children, I would literally say to

---

[32] William C. Dement PHD

myself, "I will take care of that when I get home" or "I will take care of that at 6:00 o'clock" and set it aside in my mind - vice versa, at home with work. Then I let it go.

There is no point worrying about or expending energy on things that in this present moment you can do nothing about. The only way to alleviate this anxiety is to be where you are.

Unfortunately, there is a tremendous impact on our health when we live and work with tension and hostility – with stress. The impact can be overwhelming, not only mental distraction but headaches, neck, shoulder and lower back pain, heart disease, high blood pressure, anxiety, depression, weight gain, diabetes and fatigue – to name a few!

Becoming aware of the impact that others may be having on us or conversely the destructive impact that we may be responsible for in others, helps us to focus on what needs to change. Others destructive behaviours – "transformational roadblocks" - may not be the only offender contributing to our stress.

Consider how the workplace and home life can underwrite this level of stress by an overly heavy workload, disorganization and not enough time to complete all the daily tasks. People in leadership positions contribute too – at work and at home. [33]

- 35% of those surveyed say their leaders need to set clearer expectations and provide constructive motivational feedback,

- 27% say their leaders need to admit when a mistake is made instead of blaming others,

- 22% say their leaders need to be more accessible and open to communicating,

---

[33] Job Quitters Blame Bosses Survey 2007

- 16% say that their leaders should listen more.

As leaders, if we fail to effectively deal with stress in the workplace then performance and overall productivity will suffer. As leaders, if we fail to effectively deal with stress at home, our relationships suffer.

Bullies in the Personal & Professional Realm

While some business leaders do lead and run their businesses with integrity and honesty, there are still those who have risen to the top of their professions, or organizations, over time, and have been seemingly caught in a time warp - "the bully boss" is alive and well and unfortunately still influencing the next generation.

While today more focus is being placed on bullying, specifically cyber bullying, and there are new laws to bring attention to this problem, bullying is not new. Bullies have simply found a new area to play.

Despite the fact that children are now learning about bullying in kindergarten, about what they should not do, they could also benefit from learning more on what they should do - how to manage their emotions when they feel frustrated. And, they need to learn more on how to get along with each other and how they should treat each other – about empathy and compassion.

Unfortunately, some societies still condone, even nurture, bullying. And while the focus is on what societies need to do to change – people should observe themselves – recognizing who they may have become in the process.

"Whoever fights monsters should see to it that in the process, they don't become a monster." [34]

The evidence is still all around us. We see bullies in the playgrounds that grow up to be bullies in society. [35] Some bullies lead societies; others dominate what is in their reach, their homes and or their workplaces.

Workplace bullying remains widespread. Only a decade ago, more than 50% of the calls to company-sponsored help-professionals reported abuse in work environments. At the same time - a study of one thousand workers – 42% percent reported incidents of bosses yelling and inflicting other kinds of verbal abuse. And yet, today's news is still reporting toxic work environments. A "toxic culture of fear" described as "shameful and reckless dysfunction", a board of directors that is "out of control" and "barking out orders," and seemingly, "bullying divisional workers who fear for their jobs." [36]

How does living with bullying affect our well-being and performance - as individuals, as members of families and workplaces, and as citizens?

And what does this mean for women? How pervasive is bullying in women's lives? What is the impact of it, on us as individuals and as women collectively? Do we recognize abusive behavior and, if so, what have we done about it? If we have done nothing, what stops us, and what are the results and consequences of that?

"The statistics tell us that 7% of all women are physically abused and 37% are verbally and emotionally abused."[37]

---

[34] Friedrich Nietzsche
[35] One in Seven Canadian Children between 11-16 are victims of bullies – Canadian Bully Statistics
[36] Winnipeg Free Press July 9,2015
[37] Joyce Meyer

And, while we may be under the impression that bullying behavior is exclusively a problem with the opposite sex – think again – results of the member survey indicate that women are part of the problem too! [38]

From a cross section of two hundred women surveyed on "experiencing bullying behaviours", 73 % report feeling bullied. Out of that 73%...

- 39% of the respondents advise that their bullying experience related directly with a woman,

- 62% reported yelling and swearing,

- 76% reported public humiliation,

- 60% reported being gossiped about and ridiculed,

- 70% reported being excluded or left feeling isolated,

- 77% reported disparaging remarks being directed at them,

- 76% reported they were made to feel at blame or at fault,

- 62% reported feeling targeted with unjustified criticism & fault finding,

- 60 % reported trivializing their accomplishments.

Formerly, while working in the corporate world, I am reminded of a woman who kept a book on her desk "Management by Intimidation." I expect this was an acceptable approach in her younger management years. However, it is important to keep up with progress, and as noted, women can be bullies too, not

---

[38] Survey Confidential 2003-2013 | TCC-Distinctive Voices, Dynamic Women

a title exclusively held by men. Management by intimidation certainly seems like a ridiculous notion today. Why? The act of intimidation actually stunts personal and professional growth as well as career, relationship and business performance. If people are not in control of their own behaviours, how can they be effective in their roles as leaders?

"I suppose leadership at one time meant muscles; but today it means getting along with people." [39]

However, this wasn't my only experience while working. I too worked for a "bully" who treated not only me, but other staff members - mostly women - with many of the same destructive behaviors listed in the aforementioned survey.

"It is absurd that a man or woman should rule others, who cannot rule themselves." [40]

I have also worked with some terrific leaders too, whom I continue to admire to this day.

Setbacks and Challenges

Remaining as one of the most significant challenges faced by people in today's world is "increased workloads and responsibilities" leaving some people feeling more alone and more heavily burdened than ever before!

More & more, men and women are taking on new challenges to meet work expectations and not only young family demands but blended family challenges. Furthermore, not only are people expected to "parent" their own children, they are now facing new challenges of "parenting their parents" and dealing not only with their own health issues but with theirs.

---

[39] Mohandas K. Gandhi
[40] Latin Proverb

This is leaving people exhausted and with less time to dedicate to the "care of themselves." Therefore, it is exceedingly more important to ensure that one remains healthy or they will not be in a position to adequately respond to the needs of their families and the ever increasing demands from their work and that environment.

While some people continue to put the needs of others ahead of their own, they also realize that without taking better care of themselves, they may put their personal options and desires at risk - their ability to be effective in their leadership roles as parents, spouses, partners, sons, daughters, friends and business professionals.

How do we find time? We make the time. The fact is that we all have twenty-four hours in a day. The reality is that people will do what they want to do, and not, what they do not want to do. So those excuses of "I do not have the time," "I am too busy" or "I spend all of my free time with (fill in the blank)" are no longer acceptable. Be honest. People recognize excuses!

"One always has enough time, if one will apply it well." [41]

And, it is also time to recognize the importance of keeping our personal commitments to ourselves. We can give ourselves permission to do this. While we "can do anything" we choose, we must distinguish that "we cannot do everything!"

However, while "workloads and responsibilities" are prevalent to most, there are so many more setbacks and challenges that people are plagued with in their daily lives.

People are suffering from addictions, aging issues, assault, business foreclosure and mergers, criminal behavior, deadbeat dads, death, depression, divorce, eating disorders, emotional abuse, financial stress, job loss, lack of formal education, lack

---

[41] Goethe

of technical skills, life threatening illness, mental illness, physical abuse, sexual abuse, sexual orientation, single parenting responsibilities, suicide, verbal abuse, violence, unemployment, weight issues…and the list just keeps growing.

"Be kind to all you meet because you do not know what internal battle they fight" [42]

And there are those persons who have had extreme challenges in their lives, for example, some celebrities who have had unbelievable setbacks in their lifetimes. How did they do it? How did they get through these overwhelming and difficult battles and yet, not only remain sane but rise to such personal significance? Exceptional people share common traits: patience, perseverance, optimism, preparedness. They never give up and they have incredible inner strength!

"Patience is not passive: on the contrary; it is active; it is concentrated strength." [43]

One fundamental truth to mastering emotions is an understanding of how honourable leaders move past their setbacks and challenges. They determine if the difficulty was due to them or outside of their control. They learn from their experience, understanding what they will do differently the next time. And, rather than remaining stuck and fretting about the past, they bounce back, and then, they move forward!

"In the middle of difficulty lies opportunity". [44]

And, we must not let someone else's negative thinking limit us either. Where would we be if Henry Ford had listened to Thomas Edison's suggestion to abandon his idea of a motor car because he himself was convinced that it would never work?

---

[42] Ian Maclaren
[43] Edward G. Bulwer-Lytton
[44] Albert Einstein

No one else can dream your dreams - never let others talk you out of yours.

The Demanding Years

I remarried, a man with two children of his own and in the airline industry. And although I left my career in the airline industry many years before that – I now had all the benefits! My knight in shining armor had at long last arrived. We built our dream house. I was in love. My life was a fairytale - too soon?

It never dawned on us - the unsuspected challenges that were about to unfold. We now had a blended family and another ex in the picture. More positive opinions and less controlling behaviours would have been more helpful. Never mind the trials that we endured with his children, sometimes speaking with us, but mostly, shutting us out. And there was the growing frustration my husband experienced being a step-dad to my children and his subsequent need for anger management skills. These were trying times and we were ill prepared.

My husband was living in a different city and province than I and the children were living when we met and married and although we thought that this might work, it wasn't conducive to starting a new life together. He tried to find a job where we lived but that didn't work out either. We made a decision. The children and I would move to where my husband was living. I had to leave my consulting position but I was able to transfer and remain with the same company – thanks to an understanding and supportive leader. The children and I moved onward – a new beginning.

The next few years became more disconcerting than I could have ever imagined, not only because I had a new husband, was now a step parent, had a new job, was living in a new city, had to make new friends and was building a new house but my children had a new step-dad. They were moved away from their father and all of their relatives. They had to change their school and their friends. And never mind the blended family encounters that we all had a stake in - I had a new "boss"!

While I had a couple of managers before this particular one - whom were very supportive and easy to get along with – this one proved difficult! His initial introduction to becoming the new leader was to read me and others the riot act! Where on earth did this come from? The tone was set – management by fear. The next few years would prove confounding to say the least, never mind the micromanagement.

These were hectic times for both my husband and me – non-stop working and travelling extensively. And, while I enjoyed my work immensely and we had many opportunities to travel to most corners of the world, between our children, my job, my "boss" and my husband - I felt constantly tugged in every direction. It is easy to lose oneself in the busyness of reacting to others.

"Remember always that you not only have a right to be an individual; you have an obligation to be one." [45]

After spending nearly twenty years with one company, I took a leap of faith and left the corporate world. It was with this decision and commitment that everything in my life changed - quantum leap!

At the same time, both of my children moved out to begin their own lives and my husband was required to work in a different city for a year – coming home only on the weekends. If I had known that everything in my life was about to change anyway, I may have returned to head office. Timing is everything!

---

[45] Eleanor Roosevelt

UNDERSTANDING THE IMPACT

Denial and Blame

We live in a blaming society. When we feel that someone has let us down in some way - not met our expectations - even when we have clearly done something that has contributed to the situation that we find ourselves in - we are quick to point fingers.

While in the airport, my husband insisted on carrying my computer and carry-on bags in addition to his own. He is a big strong guy so why not? While going down the escalator, he realized he needed coins for the luggage cart and let go of the computer case to get money out of his pocket. The computer bag came rolling off the last step. When I looked up to see what had happened, he said with great condemnation, "What am I, a packhorse?"

Before assigning blame, we need first to reflect on how we may have contributed to the situation! Chances are, if we had done something differently, we would have a different result. Major "transformational roadblocks" on the journey to self-discovery are denial and blame.

When you find yourself in any kind of personal or professional situation, resulting in an ending that you were not expecting, consider this. When others can see and hear from you on how you may have contributed to this end result and what you would do differently the next time, they too are motivated to consider their contribution as well. By communicating our contribution, rather than pointing the finger, we are able to calm people down, interrupt any potential conflict and argument, and engage them in conscious dialogue - bringing people back into the present moment. And in so doing, illuminate new perspectives and make way for new possibilities.

"A good leader is a person who takes a little more blame than is his share and a little less than his share of the credit." [46]

On the other hand, if we assign blame others feel put down and become defensive, triggering an emotional - angry - response. And, if this person has not yet learned how to effectually manage their anger, this emotion renders them unable to think straight. Arguments or conflict follow and they are unable to function effectively or be productive – temporarily becoming that irrational person – saying and doing regrettable things!

The same applies to criticizing, micromanaging, nitpicking and nagging – they all come across as put downs – as blaming!

When we can focus on self-discovery and developing our self-awareness, we continue to reach deeper and deeper levels of understanding of ourselves and deeper levels of enlightenment. However, the more we remember, the angrier we can become. As questions are answered, and the full realization of the impact that others may have had on our wellbeing and that of our families become known, the comprehension can be overwhelming and the blaming can begin all over again.

"Take your life in your own hands - what happens? A terrible thing: no one to blame." [47]

---

[46]   John Maxwell
[47]   Erica Jong

While we could "potentially" work ourselves into a state of anxiety and stress, knowing why we feel a certain way puts us in a powerful position to make better choices. In this "present moment" we have options: the power to forgive and move forward, to give away our power and regress or exasperate the situation and create conflict. Honourable leaders never give away their power. They are alert, aware and purposeful. They choose their desired outcome and they are open to new possibilities.

On the other hand, if in this powerful "present moment" people react destructively, they change not only their own life but that of others - in milliseconds! And when people overreact, they resort to their default behaviour.

Default behaviour can be different for each person. It can take the form of some kind of verbal or physical outburst like: crying, shouting, swearing, hitting, pushing, punching or putting their fist through a wall. For others, it can appear as though they are managing themselves appropriately because they do not say, or do, anything. They simply lower their eyes or walk away. Leaving both them and others with the impression that they are effectively managing the situation – not so!

Of-course, neither of these reactions works well for people. Any kind of outburst or loss of composure limits opportunities and changes people's perception of them. And, walking away and doing nothing, creates physiological damage – resulting in people shutting down, disengaging, becoming ill and suffering from depression and so on. So what is the answer?

When we can act intentionally and consciously - are mindful - we have the power to respond with honour. For that reason, when we can ask questions, understand from another person's point of view and appreciate that whatever was just said or done was not intended to hurt us, we can make an informed choice before we respond - ensuring that we are responding to the right intention.

When we can base our responses, choices and decisions on our desired outcome, we will begin to experience transformation. While desired outcome can be anything, for example, preserving our relationships to world peace, keeping our desired outcome in mind is an important strategy to stay connected to the present – our thinking mind – our ability to think straight.

Most of the time people are not trying to hurt others; they are only trying to help themselves! However, keep in mind that no matter what people's intention, they must still take responsibility for any harm they cause others - unintentionally or otherwise. It does not give them or us for that matter, a free pass! With bullying behaviour, harming others is their intent.

At any time, during the life span of a person's journey, they have choices. They can choose to build a better future on the knowledge and the experiences of yesterday or they can remain where they are. People can make a conscience choice to change what they can, accept what they cannot change or leave what they can no longer accept. Changing what they can also implies that they take a serious look inward – what could they, themselves, do differently?

Unconscious Choice

Anytime we have an emotional reaction, or feel that we have been hurt in some way, there is a response within us that results in an impulsive behaviour. When we feel shut down – we disengage. We feel like giving up. We just don't care. It is when people reach this state of disengagement that everything "goes out the window" and their common sense, the goals that they have been working so hard toward, disappears and they regress to their same old ways of coping - the same old rut!

"If you want to know what your thoughts were like yesterday, look at your body today; if you want to see what your body will be like tomorrow, look at your thoughts today." [48]

Whenever people feel hurt, this stressor triggers the flight or fight response, and in turn, creates all kinds of bodily changes: epinephrine and cortisol is released into their bloodstreams, their heart rate and blood pressure increases, oxygen is shunted away from the brain to their large muscles so that they are prepared for action, their immune systems temporarily shut down so the body can focus on the most necessary functions, blood sugars rise and insulin levels increase, a starvation response is triggered, cravings increase for fatty & sugary foods, and last but not least, when their bodies realize that they do not need all this energy to run away or protect themselves – it stores this energy as fat – primarily abdominal. Are you kidding me?

So while we may have great intentions - let's use maintaining or losing weight as an example - our brains are busy trying to protect us, by sending out directives that are actually working against us!

This explains why we call it comfort food. When we are feeling miserable, lonely, sad, angry or upset in some fashion eating ice-cream, cookies and potato chips makes us feel better!

However, once we are able to gain the understanding - the reason for our emotional anxiety and stress - we can assure ourselves that what we are feeling is not hunger and those cravings are not real. We can make the conscious choice when or what to eat. The next time you are going to eat take a deep breath, and stop. Are you truly hungry?

We can also help ourselves by holding ourselves accountable for what we can control. After all, the only thing we really

---

[48] Deepak Chopra

need to do is eat less and move more and for this we can be held accountable!

Oh and a couple of other things...drink water, lose the carbs, do not eat after dinner, eliminate sugar, do not eat anything white, do not eat processed foods, do not eat anything artificial, never eat carbs without a protein, eliminate salt, only eat it if it grows that way and so on and so on. That leaves meat (not red), fish, eggs, fruit, vegetables, legumes, seeds and nuts. Well so much for comfort!

Seriously, beyond someone's specific health requirements - while everything in moderation remains the key - we still need to access our common sense! And, when we are in an emotional state, we are unable to do that.

"We may have had a weak start but we can have a strong finish." [49]

With the knowledge and understanding of what is driving our emotional stress and anxiety, we can establish the right mindset, become passionate about personal change and living this passion can and will lead us to success.

And most importantly, beyond traditional coping skills, we still need willpower to overcome. However, willpower on its own merit is humanly impossible; we need "inner strength." We need empowerment!

"Be proud of today. Don't go beyond that. Don't look at how far you have to go, look at how far you have come." [50]

The importance of moving in the right direction cannot be underestimated. Keep moving, one day at a time!

---

[49]   Joyce Meyer
[50]   Joyce Meyer

Idealist Expectations

People have idealist expectations of others and when those folks fall short of those expectations - people feel let down. Their resentment grows and the complaining begins to focus on what others have, personal opinion, thoughts of entitlement and so on. People are always searching for someone or for something to make them feel better – the magic bullet!

"Fulfill me, make me happy, make me feel safe, tell me who I am. The world cannot give you those things, and when you no longer have those expectations, all self-created suffering comes to an end." [51]

Granted, some people have not been treated fairly and they have had some serious life setbacks and challenges. No one has ever said that life is fair. Rain falls on the just and the unjust, with the exception, some people will grab an umbrella!

When people have been let down, for example, when they cannot get over someone or something not being who or what they think they should be; they are unable to cope with the reality. Sadly, most people I meet through friends, coaching and workshops tell me that some kind of substance abuse or addiction has been the result - affecting their loved ones lives, relationships and careers.

Businesses too are faced with this ever growing challenge. Substance abuse contributes to higher absenteeism and presenteeism, lower job productivity and lesser performance. According to Statistics Canada; one in ten Canadians report symptoms consistent with substance dependency.

Addiction, the result of emotional pain, touches everyone's lives at home and at work - albeit their managers, colleagues, husbands, wives, parents, sisters, brothers, aunts, uncles, sons

---

[51] Eckhart Tolle

or daughters. Substance abuse and addictions stop people from living in the present. While the faces change, the stories never do - they are always the same.

"Alcohol and drug addiction are symptoms. The cause of both is intense emotional pain. When these underlying painful emotions are continually present and no effort is made to heal their causes, a dependence upon drugs and alcohol results." [52]

A woman who became divorced could not face the reality of her situation. She continued living in the past, drinking to make her days easier, until she lost her business, alienated her family and friends and eventually died alone in her sixty's.

Unquestionably, most people and family members were not as familiar with depression and addiction as they are today, and simply could not get past the rude behavior and constant need for financial help. The fact remains, that while people want their previous life style back, some people never gain the inner strength to take the necessary steps to do so. People get stuck, continuing to focus on the way things used to be, living in the past, and are never quite able to accept their reality and live in the present – their ego (personality) blocking their progress.

And yet another, when faced with thoughts about how they grew up, and reminders of their personal setbacks, turned to alcohol. Unfortunately, the same thoughts return when one is sober. Their inability to accept people for whom they are, and their focus on whom they wish them to be, keeps returning them to the past.

Most people want a better life and want others to stop judging them on their past behaviour. And generally speaking, while others are quite willing to live in the present with hope for their future, they are usually the ones who drag everyone back into the past. They are their own worst enemy.

---

[52] Gary Zukav & Linda Francis

And, there is the executive, who for all intents and purposes, had it all, and yet, was forced into retirement, lost most of his close relationships and continues to suffer from drug and alcohol addictions. There is the son who became addicted to drugs and disappeared, leaving his child to be adopted by his grandparents. There is the family man, the mom, the sister, the fiancé, the professional, the president, the business owner, the priest. The list goes on. Addiction can touch anyone and it affects everyone.

"Addiction is the continued repetition of any behaviour despite adverse consequences and it is about living in denial. Habits and patterns associated with addiction are typically characterized by immediate gratification (short-term reward), coupled with delayed harmful effects (long-term costs)." [53]

And, while people generally associate addiction with drugs, alcohol and gambling, there are other behavioural addictions that are affecting people today - the use of computers, the internet and playing video games.

How does addiction affect leaders in their roles as effective role models? How does addiction impact friends, family, relationships and careers? While so much emphasis is placed on the person with the addiction – how have friends and family members contributed?

Addiction, no matter what the addiction, does not define a person no differently than having diabetes or cancer does. They are all people with a disease, as well as, people with many great qualities and characteristics that we can admire and respect. While it can be difficult to get past those destructive behaviours, at times, it would be fitting for us to focus on and encourage all of their "progressive behaviours".

---

[53] Addictions Foundation

The fact remains that each and every person shares the same responsibility - the power to preserve or destroy, not only themselves, but others.

Addictive Behaviour

People discover that they are all asking the same questions. Why they do not have any money? Why they do not settle down? Why is everything an emergency? Why is their problem now my problem? Why does this keep happening again and again? Is everyone still living in denial?

This is not just a problem for the one suffering with addiction. Until, both those suffering with addictions, and the people invested in their well-being, accept the reality of this life threatening illness and become willing to make the necessary adjustments, the struggle, the pain and the fear will continue. Unfortunately, addiction is a family disease — there is no denying that.

"There is no growth without change, no change without fear or loss, and no loss without pain." [54]

How long should people continue listening to other's never changing stories - offering the same advice, asking the same questions, providing yet one more opportunity and bailing them out of their current dilemma - albeit financial or smoothing the waters with other friends or family members? People do this because they care but for everyone's health and financial wellbeing — it must stop. No-one can control or fix another person. This is their journey.

And therein lies the dilemma — you are trying to control them and they are trying to control you. And, whenever any person tries to control another person, or control what is not

---

[54] Rick Warren

within their control, it leads to stress – chronic stress · for all involved! Fixing other people's problems only confirms to them that they are not capable of doing this on their own and their self·confidence is once again eroded.

For that reason, people in leadership positions need to understand why they do what they do. They need to recognize their contribution to these situations and gain the inner strength to be patient, persevere and learn how to effectively manage their own challenges. And, they need to make choices and decisions based on achieving their own desired outcome.

While these types of situations can make people angry · losing one's temper will not only destroy any headway that they may have made with others, but ruin any possibility of relationship.

So where does one begin? Self·discovery and developing awareness is always the first step. People can begin by learning all the facts and accepting the reality. The next step is taking action · putting those facts to work in their own lives. [55]

As much as people want to comfort, the fact remains, they cannot help until others have the desire to help themselves. Therefore, until then, leaders must tenderly detach themselves from other people's problems and let go of their own expectations and resentments. And, they must allow both themselves and others the freedom to be as they are. If they continue to impose their ideas of how things should be, and they force their solutions on other people's problems, they only create new complications. Rather, assure others that you are confident in their ability to figure this out.

"Let them have power over their own lives." [56]

---

[55] AA and Al·Anon Family Guidelines
[56] Life Over the Influence, Kimberley Abraham, Marney Studaker·Cordner

Until individuals feel that burning passion to have a different life than the one they are currently experiencing, then all efforts are only "temporary relief" and this "crippling cycle" continues. This is not just about having willpower, it is about first understanding "what to do" or "what not to do," and then, gaining the inner strength to overcome any adversity.

Also, there are always other factors that can contribute to one's frustration. For example, in many situations, although there are usually agreements in place, others try to make new promises. However, one cannot accept promises because this is just another method of postponing pain. And, one cannot keep switching agreements. If an agreement is made, stick with it!

While our intentions are good, and we do things out of love for others, love cannot exist without compassion, justice and discipline.

Awareness brings forth acknowledgment. Acknowledgement promotes change. Change necessitates new beginnings. New beginnings arouse thankfulness. Thankfulness turns denial into acceptance. Acceptance creates a new possibility.

Inability to Say NO

The answer seems simple - just say "no"? It stops when you stop it. How many times have people given that advice to others, and yet, they continue to get caught up in the same scenario. It is not that easy, in fact, it is nearly impossible to say "no" when others are hurting. Never mind the personal challenge to say "no" to one-self.

"The more difficulty one has in saying no, the more likely they are to experience more stress - which can lead to burnout and eventually depression. "[57]

---

[57] University of California Research

It is much easier to simply fix other people's problems because then the pain goes away - at least for now - both for them and for you. It is a much more difficult proposition to hold onto this pain by saying "no". And, while this may be the greatest pain that one experiences, or endures, one can do it. And, one must do it. Changing ones attitude and approach to problems is the only recourse for recovery - both yours and theirs. Each invested person needs to feel the pain if change is to occur.

The dilemma remains. While saying "no" is the correct thing to do, people still question their decision. Minds racing with negative self-talk, wondering if this situation is their fault and is it still their responsibility to help, feeling guilty if they don't. People must not let guilt or anxiety compel them to do what others can, and must, do for themselves.

And people can make their situation even worse, and more stressful for others, because they begin to provide excuses about why they cannot help, rather than stating the obvious. In truth, until people start helping themselves, there is no point. While we - as leaders - must persist in being firm, all communication must remain kind, respectful and honest in all situations.

Despite the fact that people care for other people, they cannot support their destructive behaviors and consequently their own personal ruin. And, do not let anger get the better of you. This is not the time to blame, threaten, argue or cover up the situation. People must own their own choices and consequences.

"When you say yes to others, make sure that you are not saying no to yourself." [58]

While it is easier to say yes, and it is in our human makeup to help others, people's inability to say "no" is the lingering

---

[58] Paulo Coelho

problem. Their good intentions are prolonging the inevitable – having a destructive impact. The more people help, the more they disable.

And, while saying "no" could potentially be the progressive turning point, it now becomes the catalyst that can drive people back into the dark. Therefore, take caution, "no" must always be accompanied by something that you are prepared to do. It does not have to be an all, or nothing, scenario. And most importantly, one should always encourage any "progressive behaviours" and beneficial activities - even cooperate in making them happen.

"The journey of a thousand miles begins with a single step." [59]

Are you still trying to save this person? Do you still believe that you control other people's choices? Are they fooling anyone with their excuses – are you? Set boundaries and limits.

Emotional Blackmail

Unacceptably, emotional blackmail keeps everyone in turmoil. There is always an underlying fear of harm. The threats that keep people from knowing what they should do, but in truth, they know what they need to do. While people hope that those who are struggling will make good choices, they must be held responsible for their threats and actions and know what the natural consequences of their threats and actions will be.

And, while individuals can be fearful of losing their family and relationships, with the constant demands and the anger and guilt that ensues, it practically guarantees it. Therefore, do not let them alienate you, for then, all is lost. Those persons invested in other's well-being must remain strong for their sake - this is leadership responsibility. Never give up.

---

[59] Lao-tse

When will everyone know that progress is being made? Personal effectiveness - the defining moment - can only be measured by less frequent requests for help. For those who are helping others - when this stops too! Ultimately, we will realize transformation when people are self-sufficient and in a state of well-being.

In the meantime, people may need to forgive others over and over again for the same offence. The same offence that is recurring in one's "racing" mind. The continuing fear that grips one's thoughts can trigger their emotions and their anger can be ignited all over again. How many times should one forgive another person - as many times as it takes? Forgiveness, while it does not mean that one forgets, it does mean that one can stop dwelling on the same thoughts over and over again. One can learn from their experience and move onward!

"Courage doesn't always roar. Sometimes courage is the quiet voice at the end of the day saying, "I will try again tomorrow." [60]

The most imperative act is to recognize and acknowledge any headway, no matter how small the step. It can even help to let people know how you feel - to write them a letter.

Facing the Truth

The biggest breakthroughs usually come when people have had enough and they are feeling the most pain. Once they become aware of what is driving their emotions and behaviours - they have a choice.

"You can never find yourself until you face the truth." [61]

---

[60] Mary Anne Radmacher
[61] Pearl Bailey

When we wholeheartedly accept the reality of things as they are - stop living in denial - we are no longer held captive by fear. In fact, the fear of not doing something any longer is greater than the actual experience of not doing it.

Think about smoking, for example. The act of not smoking was not as much an issue as was the severe anxiety I felt just thinking about not having cigarettes available. It was easier for me to choose not to have a cigarette, in that moment, than to think about never smoking again. In that respect, I am still a smoker that chooses not to smoke. I stopped smoking twenty-seven years ago – one cigarette at a time - one day at a time.

When we hesitate to take the next step, or leap of faith, we can easily become discouraged, feeling as though nothing will ever change. Therefore, our attitude has a powerful effect on our ability to succeed.

"If you think you can, or you think you can't – you will be right." [62]

However, when we can truly commit ourselves, to that new choice or decision, everything begins to fall into place. All kinds of unbelievable events come about to help us, ones that we could never have imagined, even if we tried.

By choosing to live in the present: fully experiencing life, gaining the energy to enjoy each and every moment, realizing that outside negative forces no longer have any control over us, we are free. And, when one becomes passionate about this change, they gain the "inner strength" to persevere. The force to become, and the commitment to do whatever is necessary to become, is available to each of us.

---

[62] Henry Ford

Guilt and Shame

Time and time again, the right thing to do, or not to do, enters our conscious thoughts and when we choose to ignore it, and do what we want to do instead, our circumstance becomes our teacher. What lessons do people need to learn?

While there are many, the one that is prevalent to most people comes by way of providing financial support. Lending money to others is never a good idea, rather, if you feel the need to personally help someone financially, make it a one-time gift. Otherwise, if this debt cannot be repaid, the borrower is damaged by guilt. And, when the lender understands that lending money to someone who cannot repay their debts creates erosion to that person's already low self-esteem, they too become damaged by guilt.

Guilt is a feeling of regret over some action that we have taken. Guilt leaves us with a sense of obligation to make up, in some way, for the wrong that we did or imagined that we did. Even trying to make up for the damage, we feel that others have done. Are we still trying to repair wrongdoings?

"Anger is remembered pain, fear is anticipated pain, and guilt is self-directed pain." [63]

Guilt makes us overcompensate in some way, making emotional choices and decisions and not thinking straight, saying yes, when we really mean no! While our intention is always to stop the hurting, we must recognize the longer term impact. Overcompensating harms others even when our intention is quite the opposite!

On the other hand, sometimes people can be disingenuous and we can feel ashamed for what they have done. However, we

---

[63] Deepak Chopra

cannot control what others do; therefore, we should never feel ashamed for what others have done.

According to Brene Brown, Professor at the University of Houston, we are living in a world where people still use shame as a means for controlling others. "This is wrong and dangerous; shame is highly correlated with addiction, violence, aggression, eating disorders, and bullying."

Honourable leaders exert self-control, delaying gratification and avoiding impulsive behaviour that causes harm.

EXPANDING PERSPECTIVE

Teaching Our Brains

Our brains are involved with everything – what we do, how we act and how we get along with people. The brain is an organ of the human body that is totally independent. It does not need our help and is totally outside of our control. Therefore, we need to understand how we can teach our minds to work for us, and not against us.

Our brains are different than other organs in our bodies because they continue to grow and develop for our entire lives. They are continually building new neural pathways while other pathways – no longer in use – dry up and disappear.

When we hear people talk about muscle memory, they are really referring to doing something over and over again until it becomes an automatic response or we no longer have to think about it.

When we learn to swing a golf club, once we understand the mechanics of it and we practice those mechanics over and over again, it can feel more natural than it did when we picked up a golf club for the very first time. Likewise, if we are learning to play the piano, once we understand the technique, what we are supposed to do with our fingers and hands, and we practice, we can then play the entire piece without sheet music – pretty amazing.

So muscle memory is not in our arms, hands and fingers, it is in our brains. And, when we think about something, over and over again, our thoughts are actually building memories in our brains – new habits - new neural pathways. What a concept, simply practice your golf swing by thinking about it!

"We are what we repeatedly do. Excellence then is not an act, but a habit." [64]

Why do some people persevere while others give up and never achieve what another has been able to? The only thing that changes a person from a piano player to concert pianist is ten thousand hours of practice. And, developing a new behaviour is no different! Therefore, if we want to master anything, we must be willing to first understand the "how to" and then "put in" the time. It is as simple as that.

And, it doesn't matter how young or old we are, no more excuses! The good news is that we can continue to learn and develop new habits. As a reminder, it only takes twenty-one days to create a new habit – good or bad - and build that new pathway. Our thoughts are continually building memories.

However, negative thoughts create toxic chemicals, blocking the growth of new pathways. One way to reduce those chemicals and begin to grow new neural circuitry is through forgiveness, gratitude and appreciation. Keep in mind, negative thoughts also tend to blow things out of proportion and can be contagious - so even if you are the only person with a positive attitude – be the one!

Positive thoughts appear different in the brain than negative thoughts. And, while being positive doesn't deny the existence of difficulty in our lives, positive thinking releases the power of potential. Positive thinking helps us keep things

---

[64] Aristotle

in perspective and allows us to fully access our IQ and education – our common sense!

Additionally, Mayo Clinic data suggests that positive thinking can result in decreased negative stress, a sense of well-being, improved health, reduced risk of coronary heart disease, easier breathing and improved coping skills.

We need to remain open to possibility, especially when we become emotional and our perspective narrows, when we are facing yet another setback or challenge. We must, absolutely, trust that there is a better tomorrow even in the midst of our circumstances. For that reason, it is never too late to change our minds, change our thinking, change our attitude and change our habits!

"Your character is the sum total of your habits." [65]

However, our minds have been pre-programmed and conditioned with established traditions and attitudes. These are the beliefs, thoughts, ideas and opinions that we have concerning ourselves and others - formed over time - from parents, education, society, religious training, personal observation and experience. And people agonize, "you made your bed now lie in it," "be seen and not heard," "married for better or worse" and so on.

Therefore, based on our life conditioning, traditions, programming, environment and personalities, we may be our own worst enemy. In fact, we may be the one's responsible for limiting our own progress, happiness and success – remaining stuck – not making those necessary changes.

"When it comes right down to it, how many people speak the same language even when they speak the same language?" [66]

---

[65] Rick Warren
[66] Russell Hoban

In any case, no two brains contain exactly the same meaning for any word, expression or concept. The meaning is entrenched in the people, not in the words.

Managing Stress and Anxiety

Most people experience stress and anxiety from time to time, for example, worrying about finding a job, feeling nervous about leaving home or being embarrassed in certain public situations. Stress can be triggered by an event that makes us feel frustrated or nervous and anxiety gives us that feeling of fear, worry or unease. When we are feeling overwhelmed, it is easy to forget that we have choices.

"The strongest principle of growth lies in human choice." [67]

These certain bursts of stress - fight or flight, the most ancient human impulse - can produce both physical and physiological symptoms and explain why, at times, we are not feeling well. Chronic stress - on all the time - has a devastating effect, making us more vulnerable to serious disease. This ancient part of our brain contains the "amygdala" – the site of emotional learning, where the fight or flight response resides. It answers the question, "do I eat it" or does "it eat me". It remembers every emotion that we have ever experienced, and is always on guard for something that could potentially harm us based on that past experience.

If a similar circumstance repeats itself, then we get a warning – a sensation, a gut reaction. For example, this has happened to me before and I was hurt, therefore, I must run away quickly or I must protect myself.

A young woman was in a car accident, a drunk driver ran into her in an intersection. A number of things are important to

---

[67] George Eliot

note and among the most important is that she was fine – a few bumps and scratches – thank goodness. However, it took her a long time to approach an amber caution light without an immediate feeling of fear · of being hit again by another car. She physically had to tell herself – her amygdala · that she was okay and that nothing was wrong – calming herself.

Quite frankly, the same thing happens to me whenever the telephone rings, in the middle of the night, an immediate sense of fear that someone has been hurt.

The amygdala works in the dark following directives, its job is to warn us of potential harm and protect our well-being. It cannot tell the difference between something happening right now and a past experience – it is all one and the same.

While the amygdala allows us to learn, for example, if we were being chased and stung by an angry swarm of hornets, we would instinctively respond and run the next time we saw one. As a child, I sat on a fallen tree trunk to pick some blueberries, home to a hornets nest. I did not know that I could run that fast. True story!

Nevertheless, because of this unique warning ability, it can also warn us about other people. If we meet someone, that reminds us of someone else that may have hurt us in the past, consciously or unconsciously, we are immediately wary of this person and may act in unfriendly ways toward them. And then, that person's first impression of us is not the best. This negativity becomes mutual. And, while meeting this person may very well have been an opportunity, we will never know!

"I do not like that person; I should get to know them better." [68]

---

[68] Abraham Lincoln

And of-course, the opposite is also true. When we hear a piece of music, it can immediately bring us back to a wonderful time in our lives.

This site of emotional memory – the amygdala - has recorded all of our experiences that made us feel happy or sad, angry or pleased, safe or fearful and so on and raises other questions. What emotions are being recorded when children overhear their parents arguing? What experience is the amygdala having when children are playing certain video games or watching horrific movies?

The amygdala warns us of imminent harm based on our emotional history. And, this explains why certain behaviours, while they may affect some people, will not necessarily have an effect on others – it is not recorded in their emotional memory bank.

While the amygdala – site of emotional memory - was well intentioned and was well designed for ancient times, there are no sabre tooth tigers roaming the streets today. However, there are so many other stressors in our daily lives. If the amygdala is left unmanaged, it responds in ways that harm or negatively impact both ourselves and others. Yes, why smart people say and do regrettable things, or beyond that, why they overreact – cry, swear, yell or hit something or someone. Never mind the chemical effects and the impact to everyone's health.

"It is the elegance of our emotional expressions that create healthy relationships." [69]

If we do not learn to manage our emotions, then our emotions will, more than likely, manage us. Nevertheless, we can learn to recognize when our emotions are getting the better of us, and we can learn to manage ourselves and the emotions of those around us. We can create new ways of responding

---

[69] Michael Rock

and we can build new habits. New habits are developed by practicing them, by exercising them! Exercise requires discipline and self-control.

According to Harvard Business Review on Social Intelligence, an interesting and recent discovery in behavioural neuroscience is the identification of mirror neurons. When we, consciously or unconsciously, sense someone else's emotions through their actions, our mirror neurons reproduce those emotions. Collectively, these neurons create an instant sense of shared experience – whether that experience is a good one or bad one. For example, consider gang actions – one person influencing an entire group's behaviour!

And, this mirroring may very well explain why, for example, when someone is having a bad day or not golfing well and being very verbal or physical about it, others will have a very difficult day or challenging game too. Consider the behaviour of professional golfers on occasion – throwing their golf clubs or swearing out loud - and the impact to the other professionals they are golfing with. It is a struggle to remain upbeat, focused and productive under these conditions. Never mind the fact that they are "global" role models.

Mirroring behaviour also speaks to the importance of remaining positive in trying circumstances, for example, dealing with "difficult" people or "difficult" customers and the subsequent impact on employees or personal and business relationships.

There is also a subset of mirror neurons whose only job is to sense other people's smiles and laughter, motivating people to smile and laugh in return. Easily tested on a baby, smile and they smile back.

These contagious positive and negative emotions spread at fast speeds - in milliseconds - below conscious awareness. Therefore, we need to be aware of which ones we are spreading at home and at work and why dissonant or resonant leaders make all the difference. Consequently, it is imperative that we have resonant leaders guiding families and businesses, and countries for that matter.

Controlling Racing Thoughts

Have you experienced random thoughts and memories that will not stop – a disorganized mess that can leave you exhausted? Racing thoughts are common, when people are facing some kind of stressor or experiencing anxiety and worry in their lives. Those racing thoughts can be confusing and distressing, hindering one's ability to accomplish daily tasks – keeping one distracted.

These thoughts can completely take over our consciousness, this background noise can separate us from our ability to concentrate or even sleep. These repetitive thoughts, images, music and voices increase their momentum in our mind - until it is overwhelming.

As our emotions are triggered, if we have not yet learned to effectually manage ourselves, we react or overreact losing access to our intellectual mind and working memory. This results in less perspective, less good judgment and less self-control. The loss of our ability to remain in control and maintain perspective is a dangerous combination. Not only are we unable to access those two vital "progressive behaviours" for success - impulse control and empathy - but we begin to make mistakes.

"There is a big difference from having a fleeting thought and turning it into action." [70]

---

[70]   Deepak Chopra

Over time, these cumulative errors can lead management to question employment options. However, the most depraved behaviour that takes place, during all of this, is our belief that what we are thinking is absolutely right – a fatal position! Understanding that we cannot trust what we are thinking in times of stress and anxiety is important for our sanity, integrity and success. Therefore, if we cannot trust what we are thinking in this "emotional" moment – do not make that phone call – do not send that email – do not express yourself on social media! In fact, never communicate anything that you would not want printed across the front page of a newspaper or a computer screen! The unsurpassed method of communication is sticking to the facts and leaving emotion out of it.

Have you noticed when someone is losing control how their body and language changes, their tone of voice? They cannot think straight and they overreact – reduced to their default behaviour! In this "emotional" moment all personal freedoms are lost and people say and do ill-advised things.

You may not yet be able to bring your unconscious mind activity into awareness as thoughts, but it will always be reflected in the body as an emotion, and of this you can become aware." [71]

Career limiting moves are born in this "emotional" moment. During a boardroom discussion a highly respected scientist lost control, sprung to her feet, lunged at the table, told everyone what they could do and then slammed the door behind her. When we over-react to a situation, it can turn to hostile physical or verbal outbursts. How might others perceive you when you lose control? How could this affect your relationships, your career and your life?

Some psychologists suggest that we have sixty thousand random thoughts a day when our minds are in "racing" mode, unfortunately, 75% of those thoughts tend to be negative. They

---

[71] Eckhart Tolle

suggest that 40% of those sixty thousand thoughts are about the future, so we are worrying about things that haven't even happened yet, and 99% of the time, those things do not come to fruition in any case. Also, 30% of those thoughts are about the past - things that are already over. 12% of those thoughts are about self-doubt. And yet another 10% is consumed worrying about our health.

"Unease, anxiety, tension, stress, worry – all forms of fear – are caused by too much future, and not enough presence. Guilt, resentment, grievances, sadness, bitterness and all forms of non-forgiveness are caused by too much past and not enough presence." [72]

How much time does this give us to actually be focused in the present moment, in reality, to be engaged and aware of what is going on around us? To be connected? It is a waste of our valuable time. This internal dialogue, not only creates doubt in our minds, but sets us up for a specific outcome – a self-fulfilling prophecy!

During periods of extreme stress, when you are experiencing "racing" thoughts, you may find it valuable to find something that you can focus on. In a way, you need some type of mental distraction, for example, like playing golf. Golf brings your mind into the present moment. Other present moment activities include yoga, meditation and so on.

While golfing or doing anything else for that matter, understand that your mind is constantly receiving your directives through your thoughts. In turn, your mind sends out signals to complete the mission. For example, you may be thinking "do not hit the ball in the pond" which the brain translates to "hit the ball in the pond". So always think in terms of what you want to happen and not the other way around!

---

[72] Eckhart Tolle

"Worrying is like sitting in a rocking chair, it keeps you busy but it doesn't get you anywhere." [73]

Worrying, excessive self-criticism or negative self-talk tends to focus on our failures, and over the long run, studies show that it is associated with higher stress levels and even depression.

Listening to Our Hearts

According to the experts, a signal is generated from our hearts that goes directly to our brains. This signal tells our brains whether to create life affirming or life denying chemistry in our bodies. Hence, there is a constant dialogue going on based on what we are feeling. Yes, according to the phycologists, we feel before we think!

It has been said that the Heart Math Institute has identified an electromagnetic field that surrounds the heart. They suggest that this field extends for at least five or six feet beyond our bodies. This proposes that we have the ability to affect others. This also suggests others are having an impact on us too - affecting how we feel! For this reason, it is not only important to remain upbeat ourselves but to be around people that energize us!

"It is better in prayer to have a heart without words than to have words without heart." [74]

Your heart also represents the source of all your motivations – what you love to do and what you care about most. The heart reveals the real you, who you truly are, not what others think or perceive you to be or what your state of affairs force you to be.

Instinctively, we care, are passionate and focus our attention on some things and not on others - this is an indication of our

[73] Joyce Meyer
[74] Mahatma Gandhi

purpose in life. When we are on point with our purpose, we are enthusiastic! When we are doing what we love to do, no-one has to tell us what to do, or motivate us. We would likely do it for the pure enjoyment, even if we were not getting paid to do it!

The opposite is also true, when we do not have the heart for what we are doing, we are easily discouraged. And, people rarely excel at tasks that they do not enjoy doing, or feel passionate about.

How important is it to align what people do best with tasks assigned in an organization? In a world of employee disengagement, it becomes especially important. Otherwise, coupled with difficult to work for leaders, it makes the recipe for personal effectiveness and best performance nearly impossible. The best performers, in any field, are those that do what they want to do because of their passion, and not from a sense of duty or profit. When you can do things with all your heart, you can achieve incredible things.

"Aim for the moon, even if you miss; you will still land among the stars." [75]

Are you still working in a job you hate, so that someday, you can quit and do what you love to do? Are you settling for a yielding life of existence? Aim for a great life.

Renewing Our Minds

Without regular and periodic renewal experiences, chronic stress will make our performance non-sustainable and our lives unbearable. So what can we do to reverse the damage that stress is causing?

---

[75] Norman Vincent Peale

Some "in the moment" activities can control immediate stressors, for example, deep breathing brings oxygen back to the brain, counting to ten gives a person time to refrain from overreacting, removing oneself from the situation or going for a walk gains composure, taking a five or ten minute meditation break gains perspective, having a mindset of appreciation and gratitude reverses the chemical responses, and asking questions before responding assures the correct intention.

There are four key experiences that have been shown in published studies to change the impact of chronic stress – mindfulness, hope, compassion and playfulness, according to Dr. Richard Boyatzis. These are the same ones that enhance relationships.

Mindfulness is about being in the present moment. Compassion is about going out of your way to help others. Hope is about having a positive attitude and an expectation of a positive outcome. Playfulness is about laughing with others. Renewing your mind is not a one-time event, but a lifelong process.

The Country Club Years

It was at this time, although my husband had a golf membership elsewhere for many years, I made a decision to become a full member at, what most folks would consider the most prestigious golf and country club in the city. I had a number of friends there that I had met over the years and my husband was, after all, working in another city. Who could have imagined joining this club on my own merit?

Reflecting on my previous corporate interactions with this club, I thought about the first time I had walked up the steps. I had the opportunity to conduct business meetings at many golf and country clubs, on behalf of the company that I was working for. However, when I went to this most prominent club for my business meeting, to my utter embarrassment, I was not allowed to enter – lounge of sorts – men only. I couldn't believe it!

I never imagined that there were still places where women were not allowed. Eventually, when the club changed to full memberships with lounge access, rather than men and women memberships, I and another woman became full members.

While I liked the idea of being a member, and it represented what I had considered a personal accomplishment, I really did not make the time for golf. When grandchildren arrived on the scene, my priorities changed.

When I decided to leave the corporate world, I finally had time to reflect and do some soul searching – what was I going to do now?

"What the mind can conceive and believe, and the heart desire, you can achieve." [76]

I was in a position to choose whatever possibility I wanted, and so, my "mantra" became "be the change you wish to see in the world". My personal vision: to have a positive impact on others through shared experience and expertise. This vision, for whatever I was going to do with myself going forward, would need to include:

- Sharing my life, work challenges and successes,

- Being an advocate for women,

- Provide me with flexibility, not being tied down to any one location,

- Opportunity and time for golf,

---

[76] Norman Vincent Peale

- Ability to continue to travel and explore other cultures and

- Become a motivational speaker – getting paid for it might be nice!

And, so it began…

The idea that we should all share what we know with others versus waiting a lifetime to finally learn it. To find a way that would allow each of us to cut to the chase – if only I knew then what I know now!

After one year, The Country Club: Distinctive Voices, Dynamic Women™ · the online network was launched. At the same time, this created a new possibility for me – to become a speaker, coach and consultant and without comprehending it – an entrepreneur!

"If you want a quality, act is if you already have it. If you want to be courageous, act is if you were – and as you act and persevere in acting, so you tend to become." [77]

And, being that I was now in my country club years; it seemed appropriate that this online network would be an extension of that. Give all women an opportunity to belong, learn, share, connect, and contribute at the country club – of sorts!

Without the support of my husband I would not have been able to focus on this extensive project, never mind stay the course and build a business, and do what I felt moved to accomplish. However, it wasn't without challenges – in 2002, so much was new and changing in the world of technology and my knowledge of the internet, and all things connected to it, was exceptionally limited.

---

[77] Norman Vincent Peale

Communicating my ideas to graphic designers and techs about creating an online interactive website was one thing, but a leadership coaching practice and a networking "safe" place for women was unheard of. We persevered and finally launched in May 2003. Although, the practice has evolved to what it is today, we continue to send out weekly leadership messages to thousands of people globally – both men and women.

As it turned out, by the time my husband was ready to retire, my business was keeping me busy working full time! And his dream for me to work for ten years, after he retired, is quickly coming to fruition! What was he thinking?

ACHIEVING BEST PERFORMANCE

Being Emotionally Intelligent

Emotional intelligence is the capacity we have for recognizing, managing and motivating ourselves and our own emotions so that our feelings are expressed appropriately and effectively. And, it is about managing and motivating the emotional environment around us and the connections we make, with those we work with and those we live with.

"Emotional Intelligence affects how we manage behaviour, navigate social complexities and, make personal decisions that achieve positive results. EQ is one of the biggest drivers of success in leadership positions." [78]

Constant, often dramatic, change and conflict in our larger worlds demand that, while we strive to grow more centred in ourselves, we must also adapt to ever-changing circumstances external to us.

This certainly holds true in our professional lives where, across the board, beyond the traditional competencies of intelligence (IQ) and well-developed technical abilities, these other skills and abilities are seen as critical.

Research suggests - as indicated in Daniel Goleman's book on Emotional Intelligence - that in hundreds and hundreds

---

[78] Dr. Travis Bradberry

of different jobs - across a broad spectrum - intelligence (IQ) and technical skills alone does not make for best performance. EQ is twice as important as IQ & Technical skills combined. However, for people in leadership positions the importance of EQ rises to 82% versus 17% for IQ & technical skills.

While IQ and technical skills remain key; increasingly, they are seen as "threshold qualities." That is, we need them to get the interview or do the job but they alone will not result in best performance. It is widely agreed that what creates best performance is the add-on to these threshold qualities.

As emotional intelligence is the ability to manage intelligently our own strong, perhaps negative, emotions – and to understand and deal intelligently with the emotions of those around us - put simply, poor emotional management is what makes smart people do destructive things: for example, saying or doing something we regret seconds after we've said or done it, being caught in a spot where we "couldn't think straight." We have all been there.

Therefore, emotional intelligence is about managing and moving past the need for such counter-productive behaviours. Not only can EQ be learned but also, once learned, it can help us personally and professionally to make better choices - even in the heat of the moment - and more informed decisions.

For instance, decisions are based 80% on emotion and 20% on reason; therefore, it is imperative that we make decisions purposefully and that they are based on our desired outcome. These better choices and decisions, in turn, help us to improve performance – whether at home or at work – and free us to lead more fulfilling personal and professional lives. Achieving best performance has to do with self-awareness, authenticity and honest communication.

Using EQ is about resilience in the face of setbacks and being aware of the emotions underlying our behaviours. It is openness to feedback and an ability to empathize with others – not about shutting them down or turning the issue around to being "about me" or walking away from issues frustrated and unsatisfied.

Although, it does not work independently of IQ and technical skills, lack of EQ can make almost impossible the skilful management of conflicts with co-workers, team members, managers, even family. In fact, in the absence of EQ, we can sabotage our own best efforts to use our intelligence, education, training, skills and experience.

"Because of the furious pace of change associated with this economy, difficult-to-manage relationships sabotage more business than anything else. It is not a question of strategy that gets us into trouble; it is a question of emotions." [79]

Learning how to manage our emotions intelligently is not easy work. It takes courage to make this journey – but the rewards are immense. The payoff is not only in higher performance at work but also in a more purposeful and committed personal life.

"In those fields I have studied, Emotional Intelligence is much more powerful than IQ in determining who emerges as a leader. I.Q. is a threshold competence-you need it- but it doesn't make you a star. Emotional Intelligence can." [80]

The benchmark today requires a formal education in order to even get an interview and most organizations do not hire anyone without a degree. However, the fact remains, it does not guarantee that you will get the position and it certainly does not guarantee your future career success. Natural talent, education and technical ability are simply not enough. Therefore, if most people have a degree, what is the differentiating factor?

---

[79] John Kotter – Harvard Business School
[80] Warren Bennis

"If IQ tells us how smart we are, then EQ tells how we are smart; if IQ is the car we drive then EQ is how we drive the car; if IQ can get us hired, then lack of EQ can get us fired; and if IQ is like an x-ray then EQ is like an MRI!" [81]

People, relationships and organizations going through the greatest change need emotional intelligence the most!

Choosing Our Attitude

A positive attitude motivates us toward success – our lives become happier! When we are happier our performance improves, we make fewer errors and we are able to maintain our focus.

"Attitude is a little thing that makes a big difference" [82]

From a business perspective, this means fewer sick days, better customer service experiences, a better bottom line and engaged employees – a win-win-win-win scenario. In fact, for every 1% increase in the service climate, there is a 2% increase in revenue. [83] This means that the better the service provided to customers as an organization - because employees are managing relationships better and are happier - the higher the revenues earned and are contributed to the bottom line.

This explains why companies are selecting candidates with the right attitude versus candidates with only the right credentials. Clearly, candidates must first meet the requirements of the position - and given that they do – then the differentiating factor is positive attitude.

For the person – leader - responsible for hiring, the objective is to discover what "progressive behaviours" are

---

[81] Michael Rock – EQ Goes to Church
[82] Winston Churchill
[83] Daniel Goleman, Primal Leadership

most prevalent given a set of circumstances. They do this by asking behavioural based questions. These questions help discover how a person's behaviour, in a previous role or situation, could contribute to their performance in the position being recruited for.

However, even if people have the right credentials and the right attitude, it is becoming increasingly common for job applicants to lose their opportunity to join their preferred company. The recruiting company finds unappealing evidence of the person's behaviour online. Be careful of what you post online. This is anything that can be linked back to you. While legally, a company cannot use any of this information as a part of their decision making process due to privacy laws, let's not be naïve!

What behaviours are crucial to long term personal and professional success? Research tells us that the top two behaviours are self-control and empathy. Why are these two so important? How people feel about the organization, or how family members feel about their home life, can always be traced back to the leader.

"If a leader resonates energy and enthusiasm, an organization thrives; if a leader spreads negativity and dissonance, it flounders." [84]

While this means that the business can swing significantly in either direction, based on resonant or dissonant leadership within any given organization, it also means that families are in the same boat! Choosing one's attitude simply means being in control of one's behaviours.

---

[84] Primal Leadership, Golman, Boyatzis, McKee

Linking Productivity

Leadership is demanded on a personal level in our day-to-day lives and it is essential at each and all levels of every type of business or across any professional organization today. Organizations' get it – they understand that one of their crucial goals is to enhance the performance of their people. And, what generally supports performance also improves employee health and wellness – it's all connected. Take care of the people who take care of the business!

Of-course the opposite is true as well. When people are not treated with respect and dignity - at home or at work - and they become overwhelmed with the daily grind, it affects their health and wellness and productivity goes down. Clearly, work effort, time at work and work quality decreases as well as performance and commitment to the organization declines. At home, relationships suffer.

According to the Mental Health Commission of Canada, nearly a quarter of the country's working population is currently affected by mental health problems or illness leading to absenteeism or presenteeism – when employees come to work but are not really there, not productive.

Productivity, then, is driven by the leader's ability to create a work environment that encourages performance and that is why leadership competencies - progressive behaviours - cannot be underestimated. Up to 30 % of business results come from the climate that the leader creates and 70% of the climate is created by the competencies of that leader. [85] A family's well-being is created by the competencies of the role model - leader - and their ability to create an acceptable, effective and productive home environment.

---

[85] Centre for Creative Leadership

While the scope of leadership is vast - research points to core leadership behaviour that accounts for 89% [86] of leadership effectiveness: the top two are "being supportive" and "seeking different perspectives". And although leadership calls for different styles of leadership depending on the circumstance, these behaviours are the ones that are relevant to most companies today – and relevant to most families.

"The best leaders don't know just one style of leadership— they're skilled at several, and have the flexibility to switch between styles as the circumstances dictate." [87]

While research suggests, that the most effective leaders use a collection of diverse leadership styles, it is one's ability to be "flexible" that pays off in productivity and performance.

While resonant leadership is common sense; it is not common practice. When people are in a position to influence others - learning new skills and behaviours - they should find a leader who is good at it, watch that person do it, get that person to talk about how they do it, practice doing it themselves with his or her guidance, ask that person for their honest feedback, and finally, practice doing it on their own.

"Success never rests. On your worst days, be good. And on your best days, be great. And on every other day, get better." [88]

One of the most important factors of productivity and performance, at home and at work, is how well we value and appreciate people. As the biggest need people have is to feel appreciated, when we can demonstrate our appreciation for others, it not only benefits their well-being but we receive the same return on our investment. And, it not only makes each of us feel more valued, capable and respected; it gives us a sense

---

[86] McKinsey's Organizational Health Index
[87] Daniel Goleman
[88] Carmen Mariano

of fulfillment and satisfaction. This is great news. We get back what we give out!

Developing Accountability

Research indicates that successful organizations are not only creating powerful employee learning experiences but they are also focused on developing cultures of personal accountability. Why? Responsibility without accountability equals entitlement.

Leaders, who are engaged in developing accountability, are the most effective at setting expectations, when they can link productivity and performance to strategic priorities. And, why is developing a strategic plan at the fundamental core of accountability? Leaders inspire others to do what needs to be done, and without a strategic roadmap, they will not know where they are going or how they will get there.

Can you imagine setting out on a long road trip without a map or GPS? You might eventually get somewhere, but was it really where you wanted to go? Will you end up driving in circles, never getting anywhere? And, how long has this taken, and at what cost?

Leadership accountability is the most effective when enabling employees and executives to manage performance, and subsequently, when they can focus not only on the same priorities, but on the right priorities.

The same holds true from a personal growth and family perspective, it is no different, and the same rules apply. We must also learn how to coach our children, developing youngsters who are accountable for their choices, and we must let them learn from those decisions, experiences and consequences. We want our children to become leaders.

"If your actions inspire others to dream more, learn more, do more and become more, you are a leader." [89]

The magnificence of building children into leaders is dependant on the little things we do every day – molding them into the people that they will become, subsequently, that will impact our larger world. No matter what our children grow up to do to make a living, we want them to grow up to be courageous, passionate and authentic. We want their actions to inspire other people to be their best. We want them to get more out of life than they would ever have thought possible.

Setting Expectations

Parents who are fully engaged in the development of their children, who set consistent expectations and allow the consequences, will reap the rewards in the long term. And in so doing, enjoy their retirement years free from worry and regret.

"The expectations of life depend on diligence; the mechanic that would perfect his work must first sharpen his tools." [90]

This kind of focus cannot be taken lightly; this requires hard work, dedication, patience and perseverance. No easy feat for parents these days, who most likely both have to work, ensure their children are enrolled in all of the extra-curricular activities, make certain that homework is completed and know each and every one of their friends and parents.

Now we add-in the challenge of single parenting, divorce and parents not seeing "eye to eye" to say the least! And, this most meaningful profession of raising strong, independent and healthy children to become strong, independent and healthy adults becomes nearly impossible.

---

[89]   John Quincy Adams
[90]   Confucius

How important is it for parents and stepparents to get along with each other and be fully engaged in the nurturing of their children? Can parents find the strength to love their children more than they dislike their ex-partners? Everyone, with a vested interest in their children, must first agree on the importance of their welfare. Learning to work together, to ensure a positive outcome, should be their utmost goal. Consistency, among all constituents, is the key.

If you want to make progress in any area of your life, relationship or career, you need to do the right thing over a period of time, one step at a time, and one day at a time.

However, progression comes to a standstill if one takes a position of "if it is meant to be". This is a common misconception of acceptance for what needs to change. If the path becomes too difficult, rather than doing the work or making the effort to understand how one may have contributed to this situation or end result, it becomes much easier to dismiss it, and resist change. Rather, consider what you could do differently next time to get a different result. What did you learn? Or, assess the current situation, or circumstance, and plan your next move. "If it is meant to be" is a fatalist position generated from a position of denial and an unwillingness to accept any personal accountability. It is much easier for people to remain in that state of mind, to accept that they can do nothing, rather than face reality. Reality requires action.

"Change is the law of life." [91]

On the other hand, if you are consistently facing opposition to whatever you are trying to do, listen to your conscience. If you listen to what you know instinctively, it will always lead you down the right path.

---

[91]   John F. Kennedy

Communicating Strategically

How important is it to connect with people when there is a need for constructive feedback or you expect that the conversation is going to be a difficult one? Connecting with people is all about nurturing trust, fostering rapport, building bridges and giving them the gift of being fully heard. Whether you are the person delivering feedback or on the receiving end – take caution.

Take performance reviews for example. Performance reviews or appraisals are famous for negatively affecting people. The impact on the individual, and their subsequent performance, can be devastating to their careers and well-being.

According to studies, leaders can deliver an individual's "poor" performance review with compassion and motivate them to do better. On the contrary, leaders can deliver an individual's "outstanding" performance review, with a nonchalant and careless attitude, sending the message that they should search for a job elsewhere. Never mind the knockout to their self-esteem. And, according to the Wall Street Journal, two thirds of appraisals have a zero or even a negative effect on employee performance after the feedback was given. [92]

From a leadership perspective, assessments should be a formal and focused discussion with each employee, about their performance against measurable goals and objectives, to review their skills, abilities and behaviours and to clearly outline their developmental expectations. This requires an engaged leader's undivided attention and respect. However, some of the experiences being reported are: cell phones on, answering or receiving phone calls and texting during the evaluation process. Leaders are either ill prepared or not present during the process, leaving the employee with a disturbed feeling about their future, never mind the

---

[92] 2011 Work Reviews Losing Steam, Rachel Silverman

subsequent impact this result will have on employee attrition and the company's bottom line.

While companies generally have some evaluation process in place, the problem lies not with the process but with how leaders communicate the process - ensuring that all of the company expectations are actually being followed. Unfortunately, if those leaders at the top - the President and CEO - are not holding their leadership teams accountable, not only does the process not work effectively, but they are creating teams of entitlement, and subsequent stressful situations and work places.

And yet, these leaders continue to blame their teams - naïvely believing that rewarding them will fix the problem. The fact remains: until they hold their teams accountable or there are consequences for ineffective performance, nothing changes. The trickledown effect: the employee is left with the impression that the leaders of the organization do not take company processes seriously, subsequently, making that employee feel that the company is not interested in their wellbeing, or their long term development.

And of-course, human behaviour being what it is, if you do not care about "me" why should I care about "you." Employees are then less likely to be interested in the company's prosperity, and subsequently, they disengage. Bad news for the company, bad news for the individual!

"The trouble with most of us is that we would rather be ruined by praise than saved by criticism." [93]

Why the problem? Most leaders are not comfortable nor have they been adequately trained to deliver "difficult" information. With focused development, leaders can understand how to address issues effectively and appropriately.

---

[93] Norman Vincent Peale

However, while it is the leaders responsibility to spend considerable time preparing to deliver feedback or have a "difficult" conversation with others, those on the receiving end should spend as much time, if not more, preparing themselves to receive the feedback in a thoughtful and constructive way too - addressing negative issues head-on and taking the guess work out of it. This sets a positive tone for everyone involved.

Feedback or having a conversation with someone is not a one way street. "Difficult" conversations not only highlight what a person has done well and acknowledge areas of opportunity but also demonstrate what each person can do to make things better. In this way, both the employee and the leader are more likely to remain upbeat, be able to hear what each other are saying, and in the end, achieve their goals.

Communication then is the real work of leadership. You simply cannot become an honourable leader until you are a great communicator. Honourable leaders inspire people by creating real, emotional and personal connections. They have an ability to speak directly to their needs and employ communication strategy. Communication strategy is about the imparting of, or interchange of, thoughts, opinions and information by speech, writing and behaviours that involve both intellect and emotions. It is planned, intentional and purposeful and influences a preferred outcome.

How does this work at home? One could reflect on our ability to have "difficult" conversations with our children and with family members? We need to employ the same rules if we want to achieve our best on the home front. For example, there is a story of a child returning home from school excited that he had received a high grade in Science although he had received a failing grade in English. The parent's comment was about their disappointment in their failing grade, rather than their delight in the higher grade. Rather, it would be more encouraging, for them, to let them know that with the same effort in English, they could pass that too!

There are many examples of "taking the wind out of someone's sails." While golfing, one could be proud of the great drives and fairway shots only to be reminded that they had three putts! Unfortunately, these type of comments can come across as put downs – positioning others on the defensive. In fact, during a conversation, if you find others becoming defensive, reconsider what you have just communicated and correct your course. On the other hand, if you find yourself becoming defensive, it is best to ask questions, and be sure you understand, before you react.

"Be sincere, be brief, and be seated." [94]

We have all been in a position where we need to have a strategic conversation with our children, our parents, our friends, our siblings. Be prepared, be engaged, be empathetic, be encouraging and above all else, be a good listener.

Engaging People

If people love their work, home environment and what they do, then it stands to reason that they will treat people better, be more creative and relationships will improve.

"Choose a job you love and you will never have to work a day in your life." [95]

78% of business leader's rate retention and employee engagement as urgent. In fact, the issue of engaging people well is becoming one of the biggest competitive differentiators in business today. [96] The fact is that we have been talking about employee engagement for over thirty years when Gallup pioneered the concept of the engagement survey. So why are

---

[94] Franklin D. Roosevelt
[95] Confucius
[96] 2014 Deloitte Global Human Capital Trends

companies still struggling? Why are companies continuing to lose their best performers?

While the loss of best performers can be attributed to a weak performance management process and high workloads, it can also be attributed to a lack of career development and advancement opportunities.

"The role of leaders is not to get other people to follow them but to empower others to lead."

While the emotional intelligence data suggests that people leave "difficult" managers and not organizations, new research suggests that development opportunities have three to four times the impact on retention. However, while that may be true, no matter how great the development opportunities, working for "difficult" leaders can still force someone to leave, and unfortunately, for that person's own best interests that may be the right decision. Nevertheless, before making any impulsive emotional decisions, people need to carefully consider their options: how they could potentially deal with it or get over it, before making the decision to get out of it.

According to previous research from Harvard, 80% of employees were disengaged. And, while there appears to be moderate improvement, unfortunately most businesses still agree, not much has changed in the last decade. In 2014, North American Gallup statistics tell us that 69% of employees remain disengaged.

Key to understanding employee engagement is awareness of how leader's emotions and behaviours impact performance, relationships and career development opportunities. What determines their success and effectiveness is measured by how well leaders relate to others: recognize their worth, honour their word, demonstrate civility and provide progressive opportunities.

"Leaders make things possible. Exceptional leaders make them inevitable." [97]

Incorporating the Twenty-One Principles of Honourable Leadership™ into your work and home life is a powerful transformation tool.

The Twenty-One Principles of Honourable Leadership™

Honourable Leaders:

1. Demonstrate progressive behaviours to stay in the game and achieve success.

2. Adapt to situations and remain flexible in times of change and uncertainty.

3. Build relationships that are central to retention, performance and longevity.

4. Resist impulse and control their behaviour.

5. Provide clear and consistent expectations.

6. Genuinely care about others.

7. Value others unique qualities and characteristics.

8. Encourage and support others growth and development.

9. Create loyalty through engaging others.

10. Recognize how their behaviour affects others.

---

[97] Lance Morrow

11. Comprehend from another person's point of view.

12. Utilize mentors, coaches and networks.

13. Expand their knowledge and increase their perspective.

14. Address emotions that impact behaviour and drive performance.

15. Take accountability for only what they can control.

16. Bounce back from frequent setbacks, crucial to high performance.

17. Speak with the right person, at the right time and for the right reason.

18. Drive the desired outcome of their choosing.

19. Make decisions based on facts and never on emotion.

20. Listen emphatically and know when to be silent.

21. Create new possibilities by bridging understandings.

ACCEPTING THE REALITY

Sharing Knowledge

History proves that honourable leaders have a genuine interest in helping others do well by sharing what they know. By sharing our stories, experience and expertise, we can understand from each other how we have arrived at where we are today in our life, career and relationships. And in so doing, our character is revealed, our purpose is defined and we can begin to empower others.

"Everyone has a transferable commodity - knowledge. Sharing our unique expertise and making introductions for someone creates a lasting legacy." [98]

When our objective becomes more about learning who each of us is, rather than what we do, we will gain a larger perspective of how we can help others - with whom we know and what we know.

And, when we can change our attitude from what you can do for me to what I can do for you, we will discover how we can bridge people together - helping each other - to become more productive and successful. Mobilizing energies and strengths, allowing people to connect and support each other, is when we can learn and be inspired by one another.

---

[98] Marsha Blackburn

"While it is wise to learn from experience, it is wiser to learn from the experiences of others." [99]

In the same way, mentoring helps people make more informed choices and decisions for themselves by understanding real life struggles, in business and in life, from others who have been there.

"Mentoring brings us together – across generation, class and often race – in a manner that forces us to acknowledge our interdependence, to appreciate, in Martin Luther King, JR's words, that we are caught in an inescapable network of mutuality, tied to a single garment of destiny. In this way, mentoring enables us to participate in the essential but unfinished drama of reinventing community, while reaffirming that there is an important role for each of us."

Helping others, being compassionate, not only makes us feel better about ourselves, but inspires others to feel more optimistic about their own ability to achieve goals.

Creating Choices

As our choices and decisions not only impact us but impact the worlds around us, we must be cognizant that for every action there is an equal and opposite reaction. In other words, we receive from the world what we give to the world and we need to be forever mindful that we are often the cause of our own effect.

"Happiness is never something that you get from other people. The happiness you feel is in direct proportion to the love you give." [100]

---

[99] Rick Warren, The Purpose Driven Life
[100] Oprah Winfrey

Consider where you are as a result of the choices that you have made along the way. Some choices may have energized you and facilitated your achievements and success, while others have held you hostage. When you can start doing something differently than you have always done in the past, you can change the direction of your life, career and relationships. Honourable Leadership not only rests on one's ability to discover self but on one's ability to change.

"It is better to light the candle than to curse the darkness" [101]

Think about all the possibilities that are available to you and the ones that you wish to experience in your life. And, while it is easy to let one day evaporate into the next, consider this. You may be only one choice away from your better tomorrow. Have the courage to make a fresh choice today.

The Eight Resolute Choices™

1. Take action immediately, do not start tomorrow.

2. Treat others right no matter how you are treated.

3. Work on breaking a bad habit one day at a time.

4. Find new processes to work smarter not harder.

5. Make the time by scheduling what is important to you.

6. Do something helpful for someone else.

7. Live a balanced life between self, family, work & community.

8. Give more than you take.

---

[101] Eleanor Roosevelt

Time for Reflection

Despite the appearance of being successful many people are stuck and only recognize in retrospect some important indicators of their environment: dissonant leadership, emotional abuse, bullying behavior and so on. This kind of behavior can have a devastating effect on health and performance - making it even more important to recognize these situations before the damage is done. And, whether one has arrived in this place because of the behavior of others or one recognizes themselves in these roles, it may not be the only offender holding people back or blocking their success and happiness.

"Successful and fulfilled people make the time to think, plan and reflect. They are awake to their lives because they know that each day is an incredible gift. If you don't believe that, walk into a hospital on the way home and talk to someone in the cancer ward. Ask what they would give for an extra day of life." [102]

Taking the time, or making the time, to reflect on how change can be better managed by adapting personal style, accepting feedback and having a willingness to listen and learn are important steps. But it is the ability to manage relationships, without being too harshly critical, insensitive or too demanding of others, that is ultimately crucial for managing change. When one begins this evaluation, observing these characteristics of oneself, or of others, regardless of their own, or others, skill, ability and education, it may bring increased insight to their current life challenges and setbacks.

A compilation of research, personal observation and individual's experiences - The Reflection Series: New Beginnings - depict personal and professional situations that may impact or have already collided with people's lives,

---

[102] Robin Sharma

careers and relationships. And, while an individual's personal interpretations of these Reflections will be unique to their own emotional history, the inspirational messages are designed to help them define and record their own thoughts and add clarity and meaning to their own past and present lives. By helping people to understand that they are not alone and that others can empathize with "where they are at," these Reflections may help people see their own experiences in a way that will bring them into the present, equipping them to make those more informed choices and decisions.

"Experience is not what happens to you, it is what you do with what happens to you." [103]

How people see the world is how they affect others around them, so understanding and having clarity about they themselves, being able to understand from others point of view and having the ability to see things the way they actually are is when they will begin to make the biggest difference. In changing themselves, they will have a positive effect on their own worlds.

Conscious Learning

We cannot change the circumstance of our childhood, how we were treated, who our parents were, where we went to school, who we were married to, much less; improve them at this particular time. However, we can recall them honestly, reflect on them, understand them and thereby overcome their influence on us. We do not have to keep things as they are but be hopeful for things as they can be, we can actively participate in making things happen.

"I find the great thing in this world is not so much where we stand, as in the direction that we are moving. To reach the

---

[103] Aldous Huxley

port of heaven, we must first sail sometimes with the wind and sometimes against it – but we must sail, not drift, nor lie at anchor." [104]

Reflection is a way of making learning conscious. Reflection gets to the heart of the matter, the truth of things. After appropriate reflection, the meaning of the past is known and the resolution of the experience, and the course of action that you must take, becomes clear.

When you are down; think of things that you have to look forward to. When you are no longer in the grip of the mishap, then you are ready to reflect on it. Self-reflection is how we begin the process to better understand and know ourselves, and in developing this awareness of ourselves, we increase our personal effectiveness - restoring honour to leadership.

"Withdrawal can be turned to hope, compulsion to will, inhibition to purpose, and inertia to competence through the exercise of memory and understanding. The unexamined life is impossible to live successfully." [105]

We begin to reshape our world by reshaping ourselves; the question has never been about how to change others, but rather how to change ourselves – making ourselves accountable so that we are no longer held accountable by our circumstances.

Inspirational Messages

The twelve individual reflections in this "New Beginnings" series encapsulate an inspirational message and are about choice and change – reminding us to keep balance in our lives at all times. Whenever we are doing something for others, or if what we give and what we receive are perceived as not equal,

---

[104] Oliver Wendell Holmes
[105] Warren Bennis

we feel manipulated and become angry. As long as there is an equal return on our investment, we will be okay in any situation.

However, some people can become so preoccupied with their own struggles, they are not aware of the impact they are having on others. On the contrary, there are others that know the damage they are causing and either do not care, or do not know how to stop. On the other hand, honourable leaders base their responses, actions, choices and decisions not on emotion or impulse but on their desired outcome.

Therefore, the following collective of knowledge, wisdoms and experiences are shared, not as an absolute method but as a way of guiding us through a process, reflecting on what is important in life. These concise twelve reflections - vignettes - are about choice and change. They are "thought provoking," "powerful," "insightful" and "inspirational." They "tell it like it is." [106]

"All glory comes from daring to begin." [107]

Every ending represents a new beginning. Each new beginning represents an opportunity for change. Without change, we can become trapped in the past. If we remain trapped, we experience the same results over and over again. With change, there is opportunity for personal effectiveness. Real change happens when we have a willingness to learn. Our best learning comes from self-reflection. Self-reflection is the foundation upon which we build honourable leadership. Honourable leadership brings meaning and satisfaction to our lives.

---

[106] Gayle Swirski, Psychologist
[107] Eugene F. Ware

THE REFLECTION SERIES™
NEW BEGINNINGS

You Are Not Alone

This First Reflection's inspirational message is "you are not alone" and is about choice -"I can do anything - but I cannot do everything." The title of this Reflection is The Night Is Long.

THE NIGHT IS LONG

It is difficult to know when the sun went down for the very last time. Only years later, is there a glimmer of a glorious sunny day. Do you fear that you could go back to sleep at any given moment? That you must be forever on your guard because you never know who or what will present you with that sleeping potion?

Have you ever been physically ill? Do you remember how you had no energy, no desire to lift you head, get out of bed or eat? You became so tired, so weary, so horribly exhausted? An infection can come out of no-where, destroying you, before you know that you are even sick and rendering you incapable of even the simplest of tasks.

These very same symptoms can sneak up on your mind, anyone's mind, anytime. So devious is the infection of "depression" and yet, so very different from physical illness. With physical illness it is acceptable to get some rest, but when the infection is in the mind, daily routines must still be performed. Everyone's expectations – ours and those of others around us – must be met. If you are to endure, you must master the little energy you have left.

Yet, there is not enough stamina for all of the things that you must do. Not now anyway. So, what will suffer – career, children, spouse, partner, health? Subconsciously, the priorities begin. Can you become the world's greatest juggler? Are you willing to gamble? What will be the cost? Something will not survive.

You are not trying to fool anyone. After all, you are not aware you need help. You are simply trying to cope. And yet, try as you might, you keep losing ground and you find yourself trying harder.

What is wrong? You question things that do not feel right, but everyone around you denies your queries and the world becomes a very contradictory place. This very frustration makes you wearier and drives an unbelievable lack of interest in absolutely everything. Do you not have a nice home, family and profession? What is happening?

Doctor's and friends will kindly advise you that the secret to your wellbeing is exercise. But by now, your energy is depleted. Maybe tomorrow you will feel better. You will make great plans to start your new regime. You will be better organized, you will eat better and, you may even look for a new job.

Sound familiar? How do we get to such a place? How long has your nightmare been going on? Can you recall the incidents that have driven you back into the dark?

Many experts say that everything that happens to us is a result of the choices we make. While this may be true; there are many people in this world that greatly influence our condition by their need to have control over others. With this emotionally abusive behaviour, our bruises, unlike those of physical abuse, are hidden and can go undetected.

How is your health? What is your situation? What changes do you need to make?

It is with this first spark of recognition you will feel re-energized. Your strength will return. The sun will begin to rise again and with this burst of light over the horizon; the dawn of your new beginning.

You are not alone.

Be Yourself

This Second Reflection's inspirational message is "be yourself" and is about choice - "how did I lose me-how do I find me." The title of this Reflection is Crazy In The Making.

CRAZY IN THE MAKING

When did this happen? Are you crazy? You hear what is being said, but the action never matches the words. Do you believe what you are being told, or do you believe what you know to be true? Can you still trust what you feel and what you think?

It has taken a very long time, and only after similar peril befalls you yet again, does it finally click, and you realize... What possesses individuals to justify their own undesirable behaviour by developing this crazy-making attitude without any care given to the cost to anyone else? How dare they make themselves feel so good at another's expense? What lies will be told? How much will you believe because you want and need to believe?

Brenda Oliver

If only you had done this, or if only you could be this way or that way, then everything would be - or would have been okay. This is told to you, but all the while, the dye has been cast and the secret intent has not changed.

Unaware, you try to change and be who they want you to be. Give up your identity. No longer be you. You try harder and become even more determined. Can you do anything right? No matter how backbreaking it is; you glean the feeling that your effort is not quite good enough. Why are you so unhappy?

Typically, for a person to justify their own position or their decision; they must convince themselves and others that their way of thinking is the correct one. Or, they are not satisfied with their current life existence, and thus, OTHERS need to change.

Therefore, criticism becomes the daily nourishment that is doled out by the aggressor. If you can swallow enough; you will fit the design that has been custom cut to meet their predetermined needs and desires. While this may be good for them; it is not your choice. Are you not a separate and unique person with your thoughts and dreams?

This other person's behaviour may not be obvious – to you or anyone else. And for some unexplainable reason; we learn to tolerate this toxic handout bit by bit until we have a steady and regular diet. Somehow, over time, it becomes acceptable to the palate.

Then, why are we still so hungry? Can we no longer tolerate this cold table of confusion? Has it finally depleted our spirit, enthusiasm and self-confidence?

It is with recognition that you will begin renewal and smile again. Be who you were meant to be. After all, this problem was never yours.

Be yourself.

Be Strong, Move On

This Third Reflection's inspirational message is "be strong, move on" and is about change - "burning bridges - some bridges need to be burned." The title of this Reflection is Emotional Terrorism.

EMOTIONAL TERRORISM

Interestingly enough, not only with September 11th, did the full impact of terrorism finally hit home. How easy it is to forget the many faces of evil there are, where it can strike, and the fear it can invoke. Have you reached a point where every communication strikes such terror in you, that, yet again, you are frightened you will be brought to tears, made to feel deficient in some way? Finally, to question life's very existence?

The fact others (or another person) can have such control over your life is bewildering. When you realize you have somehow allowed it, you begin to question; how and why this could happen?

Consistently and over time, the face of terror assures you of more preferable times to come. So you strive to do better and, for a time, may even feel somewhat re-energized. But, over and over again, "they" take away the prize, the promise, the reward. Why can't you learn? Why don't you get it?

These events have a mind altering effect. They drive the blade of power and control deeper and deeper into your very soul. Hope and trust...is this drives us on? The desired belief, that, after all, this person does have our best interests at heart? Or, is it our shear will to survive?

Brenda Oliver

Why must this be so difficult? Do you not want to do a good job, live your life in peace? Why do others appear to feel so threatened by your very existence?

Isn't this unbelievable, instilling fear in others in order to achieve a personal agenda? What are they afraid of? Will they be exposed? By mere coincidence, has this person risen to a position of some authority and not by reason of leadership skill or significant personal accomplishment? Must he or she now continue the cover up in order to sustain their position in this organization, to maintain their control?

So, they provide encouragement. After all, this is expected of a leader. However, this type of leader provides just enough reassurance for you to perform. Not enough that you grow confident; start to think yourself too talented or, in fact, that you may have alternatives. After all, if you were to discover a more progressive avenue or develop confidence in your own ability, their power would be lost.

Is their fear then, simply one of losing control-that others may gain some advantage over them in some way? Is that what it's all about? All this time, you have worked so hard to contribute, to be recognized. Does your achievement only increase the threat to them? Does this need for supremacy, then, promote fear in others to maintain this sense of power? What a paradox – when quite the opposite is true.

Oddly enough, because of this tyranny, the very people, who could have supported that other persons' leadership, are finally shattered.

Will this breed of leader ultimately exterminate himself or herself? Time will tell. You, however, should not wait. You cannot win this battle today.

Be strong, move on.

Speak Up and Behold

This Fourth Reflection's inspirational message is "speak up and behold" and is about choice -"people do what they know - rewrite the script." The title of this Reflection is The Human Connection.

THE HUMAN CONNECTION

Where did this notion come from that it is okay to completely ignore someone? Be treated as though you were not even there? You are standing right in front of them. You can hear them. You can see them. They are not invisible. So, what is this unacceptable behaviour about?

People interrupt, turn their backs in conversation, cut others off and not wait their turn, all in a self-centered belief that their mission, or their way of thinking, is more important. Has this happened to you...in a meeting, a presentation, while driving or simply while you happen to be talking?

Is this why we hurt? Is this what makes us so angry? Simply not being seen, not being heard?

Why do people feel the need to put others down, to steal from them that moment of pleasure, of personal pride or achievement? You were feeling so confident, so satisfied. Does putting you down make that other person feel better, more self-assured? Does it help to build their self-esteem?

What of being let down by those you trust? Do you not try to provide the correct detail, offer what they ask /require, try and encourage an easier existence? Why are your efforts treated as insignificant? Where is the appreciation for your struggle and hard work? Would acknowledging your contribution make them feel less important?

And what of being shut down in the middle of a conversation? Do they need others to see how important they are or how much knowledge they have? Is it because what they have to say is so much more important than what others have to say? Are they the only ones with value? Do they actually see themselves as the absolute authority? Are they simply absorbed in their own selves / their own sense of importance? This is embarrassing for all concerned. Why can' they just stop, wait and listen?

Do you feel wounded, ill-treated or not respected? Do not live in isolation. Get connected. Your contribution is significant.

Speak up and behold.

Do Not Give Up

This Fifth Reflection's inspirational message is "do not give up" and is about change -"the time is now - to extricate yourself, to evacuate." The title of this Reflection is Corporate Cancer.

CORPORATE CANCER

This disease is slowly eating away at the life of the organization. Removing any trace of the last human element. There it is: the resounding sound of the lean, mean, functioning machine. Is it destined to be just the skeletal remains of a "cheap bully", where, a robust company once stood?

But what of the employees /leaders who are expected to deliver — is it at the expense of their values, of their integrity? Are they expendable? Are there more where they came from? Is that the strategy: to continually refill the hourglass?

And so what - does it really matter to them - as long as they have you meeting the bottom line and shareholder expectations? The company is making money. This is the ultimate, right?

What pressures does this place on leaders today? Will they have the courage, the self confidence to stay immune and act within the framework of their analytical minds, their beliefs and values? What is happening? Who are these strangers? Have they become the instruments for disseminating poison in the workplace?

What happened to the nurturing organization (the idea of taking care of the people who take care of the business)? When did they forget this basic premise?

Isn't it curious: that while they are pushing the employee population to deliver (to raise their own profiles and company profits) they are actually dismantling the very framework they were trying to build on? Yet, seemingly unnoticed, this malignancy continues.

How long will it last? What will be the final straw? When will it all come plummeting down?

Recognize the symptoms. This toxic condition will make you sick. Do you want to remain indoors absorbing the poison, never over exerting yourself, taking more and more prescribed medication? This need not be the end. It need not be terminal. You are not yet finished your epoch.

There are still organizations out there that know that a healthy employee is at the very foundation of prosperity.

Are you exhausted? Remain strong and continue to fight for who you are, for who you know you could be. It is not too late. Stay conscious.

Do not give up. It is not your time.

Recognize Your Friends

This Sixth Reflection's inspirational message is "recognize your friends" and is about choice -"the many shades of friendship - the past, the present, the future." The title of this Reflection is Here Today Gone Tomorrow.

HERE TODAY GONE TOMORROW

You will meet and make many acquaintances in your lifetime. Who of these will become your friend? Isn't it curious what circumstances bring people together and at what instant each relationship solidifies?

Some will say they have had pals for many years and never really speak to them. Yet when they do talk, it seems as if no time has passed. They carry on a conversation as though it was only yesterday. Is this friendship?

Others profess to be your confidante, calling you all the time, asking you advice, appreciative that you are always there but, alas, only when it suits them. Is this a friend?

And, what of your long established kinship with someone? Is it now set aside because a spouse or significant other diverts their attention? Is this your friend?

Finally, there are your workplace buddies. Are they not there to advise you/furnish their guidance? To empathize with you when you doubt decisions or direction? Will they still be inclined to collaborate when the journey gets severe? Is this friendship?

Do you feel neglected, not treated with due respect or consideration? Has everyone now become too busy to stay in touch? Does it matter what is going on in your life? Are you now on standby? Is it worth the struggle?

Or, are our expectations too high, perhaps, simply different than others? And, on whose value systems are those expectations based?

Friendship takes time to develop and grow, to evolve through shared life experience. It nurtures caring and trust. It is not automatic.

Who, then, are these special individuals? Do they take things personally? Do they criticize? Are they judgemental? Or, do they simply let you be-even help you be-who you are? Are you patiently waiting? Are they?

Friends are rare. Recognize them.

Be a Survivor

This Seventh Reflection's inspirational message is "be a survivor" and is about choice -"check mate versus check out." The title of this Reflection is The Victim.

THE VICTIM

At what juncture, does it finally dawn on you that you are not happily coexisting with the rest of your organization? Is it the loss of passion, just not fun anymore? Is it the lack of sleep, the exhaustion? Do you think someone is actually out to get you? What happened? Have you become paranoid? How did you end up on this track?

Brenda Oliver

You have been employed for a long time, know the business well and have always achieved and had excellent reviews, until now. Over time, you have earned the right and privilege, (or so you believe) to speak your mind. You are even considered somewhat of an authority and respected in the organization.

You have witnessed the demise of others over the years, and you think to yourself: is it not obvious? Do they not know their hour has come? It seems so apparent to everyone else.

The scenario: enter a new person with no company history, but with the authority. This new leader is probably anxious to make his mark, propose the improvement and implement the new process. However, without adequate information, he is often too quick to judge and find his players.

And, it takes only one person who has always felt threatened by you, a person weak in integrity, but able to position himself or herself as a follower. In order for this character to be acknowledged, by the new person in charge, and, now to be considered credible, he or she must be sure to charm. Opportunity knocks. They have just become the pawn.

The game begins. The challenge: to find fault with those he or she feels threatened by, to justify a conclusion, after the fact. Are you now on the receiving end of insults, denigrating remarks, threats, unrelenting criticism and intimidating behaviour? Are they playing fair? Do you know the new rules?

It reflects badly on some of our leaders today, that they give so little thought, are so unconscious, so manipulated. Why are they so eager to believe or do whatever they are told? Is it all in an attempt to save themselves, get in a position for their next move? Can they not see what they are doing? Do they even care?

Do not wait for the chase to begin. Ask for advice. Get in the game...or get out.

Be a survivor.

Stand Tall and Take Your Leave

This Eighth Reflection's inspirational message is "stand tall and take your leave" and is about choice -"the bloom is off the rose-to everything there is a season." The title of this Reflection is Over The Edge.

OVER THE EDGE

You cannot help it, but now the slightest provocation drives you to react. You seem unable to hold back. You snap. You make a mental note. You say to yourself, "no more". People are observing a transition...

Why did no one notice how badly you were being handled or see the inequity you were expected to endure? You invested a substantial percentage of your life and made significant contributions to this business. You do not wish to start over.

Is it better to get guidance than to wait until it is too late? Is stress leave the answer? But if so, what is the stigma attached to that decision? How will this impact your career? Are you still under the impression-believe-you can still manage, are still capable?

What held you back from speaking up earlier? Are you not expected to challenge up to more senior leaders? And, if you had, would it have made your life any easier? If only this were the case. You are at their mercy.

An outsider drinks it all in, grasping only the impertinence, impatience and lack of flexibility you now display. It is easy for them to be judgemental. They cannot appreciate or untangle the saga that delivered you to this point. Perception is reality.

What are you to do? Spend your time focusing on how and why this isn't fair? Then, what is the answer? What should you do? Is day to day survival getting harder?

Are your daily business challenges nothing compared to the constant harassment, daily criticism, and abusive behaviours you are subjected to? You are fighting the enemy - one that will keep you distracted, overcome and off-balance.

How can you continue? How long will you last? Will your work or your home life suffer? Are you now contributing to your own demise?

Companies will not make it straightforward. They do not want to lose a top performer. How would that reflect on management's abilities? It is more difficult, time consuming and costly for them to deal with the truth. They would rather call it a performance issue. Have you now complied? Management can more readily come to terms with this kind of departure.

Do you feel doomed? Wake up from this nightmare.

Stand tall. Take your leave.

Believe in Yourself

This Ninth Reflection's inspirational message is "believe in yourself" and is about choice - "an opportunity for creative change." The title of this Reflection is Your Choice, Your Destiny

YOUR CHOICE, YOUR DESTINY

Your day has come and it is devastating. This was not part of your original portrait-your plan-perhaps someday, but not now. Not like this. Some of your acquaintances have left this organization, but you are not prepared. Although, here you are. Was this genuinely your decision? Realistically, were there alternatives?

You have been placed in a position that requires you to explain your departure. And you hear yourself saying the words, "All the new possibilities...it is very exciting." And you persist... "what a tremendous company to have worked for. You talk about it-how you loved what you did. Are they convinced? Are you?

After all, you had many opportunities to encounter so much humanity, both in your own organization and your business community beyond. Some will remain lifelong friends. You take this moment also to appreciate your teams over the years. And for all of this, you are truly grateful.

But if, for the most part, this is all valid, then why are you still distressed? Did you really have a choice? Will you go on brooding over the injustice? Does your memory continue to regurgitate the detail? Was there an option? If you had elected to stay – would this have meant your undeniable destruction?

Others will tell you, you have been handed a gift. You can now discover your passion. You can now take time for yourself. This all reverberates like a miraculous fantasy. Why, then, are you still haunted by this dramatic shift? Life altering experiences are not fair.

However, our own life histories prove time and time again, that when one door closes, another one always opens. You will look back on these events, and, when you do, you will wonder why you put off making your decision for as long as you did?

You may even feel thankful that you did not waste any more of your time in that place.

Trust that your world can be transformed into a more worthwhile place.

Believe in yourself. It will happen.

Choose Your Destination

This Tenth Reflection's inspirational message is "choose your destination" and is about choice -"at a crossroads." The title of this Reflection is Metamorphosis.

METAMORPHOSIS

Are you at a point where you wonder what you are doing with your life? Is this the only avenue open? Can you endure, or will you simply slip away? Have you struggled with this dilemma over the years? Do you feel stronger now? Is the fog finally lifting enough that those pitfalls are now visible?

For the most part, onlookers would surmise that your life is first rate. The children are now young adults and on their own. You have the opportunity to relax and enjoy life.

Blah, blah, blah...something is still not right. Can you feel it?

Does the emotional past continue to haunt you? With what now appears to be little provocation, does the floodgate open and immediately overwhelm you with that same old depressed state of mind?

Will others ever understand how their outbursts affect you and those around you? Can they not see that their miserable behaviour disturbs everyone? Is this an attempt to be funny? Is anyone amused?

The lacking in tolerance, the clear displeasure exposed by their eyes, but why? Can't they understand how distressing this is? Where is the caring? Where is the common courtesy on display for any stranger?

What about your children? When they hurt, do you hurt? If they are treated with unkindness, do you feel it too? Mothers and their children are not separate entities. They are one. They are absolute.

How then can these people tell you they love you one minute and the very next instant deliver you to the very depths of sorrow and regret?

We all deserve to be treated with respect. It is not okay to abuse or to be abused in this fashion.

Yet here you are, expecting to reach an altered state but persisting in travelling down the same path. Has the hour come to opt for a different route?

Change requires desire and acceptance of the responsibility.

You have the strength. Choose your destination.

Focus on Your Dreams

This Eleventh Reflection's inspirational message is "focus on your dreams" and is about choice -"achieving emotional balance" The title of this Reflection is Held Captive.

HELD CAPTIVE

It is virtually impossible to slow down your pace once you are on this treadmill of accomplishment and expectation. And, it is simply too exhausting. Does one day evaporate into the next? Before you know it, there you are, merely flickering.

You become and remain industrious. You wrap yourself in as much activity as you can grasp, so you can avoid the painful memories-past and present-that endlessly haunt you, always lurking, always waiting.

Most people will focus on their house of work. For others it may be golf "or a similar distraction," exercising to the extreme –or over indulging – in some other way; just as long as you stay too preoccupied to permit your brain the luxury of feeling and thinking.

If you did allow yourself to drift back into the past, what brand of pain would surface? What are you afraid of? Would your comfort zone disappear? Would you not be able to function effectively? Would you crumble? And, would you feel the need to launch into a draining internal debate on why life is not fair or, on where you went wrong?

Have you been adapting your life and making decisions based on your emotional history rather than your desired outcome? Has this plight already paralyzed you? Made you incapable of progress? Do you incessantly discover yourself in the same difficult circumstance over and over again?

Living in this fashion only consumes what precious time we have left.

The only way off this merry-go-round is to acknowledge those painful memories and events. Label the emotions. Feel the anxiety. Experience the tears. And, comprehend the remorse for what might have been.

Now, enter into those courageous conversations with yourself - or with others – that you need to have in order to get closure. Bet then, let it go.

Your spirit will rebound. Your course will become clear.

Re-focus, this time on your dreams.

Experience Your Life

This Twelfth Reflection's inspirational message is "experience your life" and is about change -"the growing pains in self-reflection." The title of this Reflection is Lonely Days And Lonely Nights.

LONELY DAYS AND LONELY NIGHTS

Are you merely existing-not really living-inside your own secret nightmare, yet always awake? Eventually the days and nights cannot be separated from each other. Are you asleep or awake? How can you be sure? What does it matter? No one notices?

It appears inconceivable you survived that time. Looking back, it was like being in a trance, the endless sleepless nights... migrating through the dark until dawn. All the lonely hours, with only your own tears and breaking heart to keep you company.

To feel so forlorn is terrible. Even more bewildering is to feel so solitary while surrounded by your family. You all live together, you eat together, although it is true everyone is engrossed in their own lives and individual activities. So what is the issue? Why this overwhelming feeling of despair? Have you ever felt so alone? Why do you feel this way?

Are you getting any sleep? Do you feel sad most of the time, or have difficulty concentrating? What happened to those happier times? Where did the excitement, the passion go?

Sharing a house is not the same as sharing a life. Is everyone too busy or simply too tired? Does anyone even care? Are you still in love? Is there still love? Everyone is here but not really present. Is anyone talking? Is anyone listening? Is anyone breathing?

Gradually, and over time, the passion disappears, and the love is held in check. You instinctively know something is wrong and you notice aspects of your relationship are changing. When you try discussing your concerns, all you receive is denial. Finally, one day you feel utterly alone, bereft. Places once stirred with desire and tenderness now lies captive to sadness and depression.

Withdrawing and holding back in any relationship is not acceptable. Given that there is no other outside influences... then perhaps this is the last frontier for that person or those people who are still caught up in their own need to exercise control over whatever and whoever is available.

Are you barely holding on? Can you live like this? The decision is yours.

Life is all around you. Experience it. Feel it.

COMMITTING TO ACTION

Defining Success, Achieving Significance

Harvard Business School considered two specific areas for defining future success, how well individuals do professionally in their career performance and how well individuals do personally with the longevity of their relationships. By this specific definition, it is easy to consider both ourselves and those around us - colleagues, friends and family - and to quickly judge who has been successful and who has not.

However, this is not the only measure of a person's success. How do you measure success? What does success mean to you? How or when will you know that you have achieved personal success?

Although, success is typically defined by what we have, how much money we make or what we do for a living, success can be better defined by whom we are. Success, then, is more about how we have positively influenced others and how we have made a difference - working towards a more "significant" personal and professional life - that which we can become!

Developing a Personal Philosophy

Discovering a personal and honourable leadership philosophy helps us to achieve a more successful - significant - personal and professional life. While each leader should take the time to formulate a personal philosophy that defines how they wish to live their own lives - personally and professionally - these fifty-two philosophies can serve as a guideline when they, as honourable leaders in their own worlds, are faced with choices and decisions.

Use these Fifty-Two Honourable Leadership Philosophies as your confidential guide. Begin by defining who you actually are today versus that which you will become – reaching your full potential - your best self.

Reflect on one principle each week, focusing on the following questions with respect to these three categories: Behaviour, Leadership, and Performance.

- What feelings arise and what thoughts come to mind when you read this principle?

- What changes will you make to bring about your best self?

- Outline the actions that you will practice each week, at home and at work, to remain focused on the particular philosophy that you have chosen to work on.

- At the beginning of the following week, reflect on your previous week's journal entry.

- Record the insight that you have gained and the change that you experienced.

- Note your positive results.

- After fifty-two weeks define your own personal philosophy.

"I find that the great thing in this world is not so much where we stand as in what direction we are moving." [108]

We gain greater insight and clarity about our lives, careers and relationships when we are able to capture our thoughts, emotions and ideas by writing them down. Otherwise, these thoughts may only exist for a fleeting moment, and consequently, this directive and useful information is lost.

The Fifty-Two Honourable Leadership Philosophies™

1. **Be yourself and never pretend to be someone that you are not.**

    When you try to be someone that you are not to try and please others, it creates tension - pushing yourself to think in ways you do not think, acting in ways you do not act or doing things that you do not do. As this behaviour is generally unsustainable, it increases opportunities for failure. The further you push yourself to be someone that you are not, the more painful your fall back to reality will be.

2. **Know that you are not alone and that we all share the same frustrations and challenges.**

    It is easy to forget that others are suffering with similar setbacks in their lives, relationships and careers. By sharing stories with each other, it helps not only to build empathy – a key component to success - but brings people together and alleviates loneliness.

---

[108] Oliver Wendell Holmes

Brenda Oliver

3. **Act in win-win ways, helping others to succeed.**

Win-win solutions are the most desirable way to solve problems and conflicts. However, you must be careful that negative emotions: the fear of losing, the anxiety of not finding a way out or your anger at the other person does not manifest itself. When both people can win, rather than a winner and a loser, then the relationship grows stronger.

4. **Be confident that you can do anything and understand that you cannot do everything.**

This problem does not lie in your inability to accomplish whatever you set your mind to do but in your ability to remain focused. If you take on everything that is coming at you, you lose your capacity to respond appropriately and effectively. There will always be more to do than you will have time to do it.

5. **Under promise and over deliver, giving more than anyone has a right to expect.**

This practice allows you to follow through on your commitments, building trusting relationships and respecting others time. Building a contingency into a plan is prudent to ensure that you do not let others down. Consider the impact you could have on others if this was reversed – if you over promise and under deliver?

6. **Build relationships by knowing who people are versus what they do or what they have.**

When you care about people as individuals, they are far more likely to give everything they have to help you. They will be happier themselves, and subsequently, contribute more to the business, family dynamic or relationship.

7. **Dare to be different, moving in the direction of the unknown.**

It is okay to be different and walk your own path holding your head up high, not compromising your beliefs and earning the respect of others. Go outside the box. Faith requires mobility.

8. **Be well informed before taking any action.**

Many people make choices and decisions based on very little information or react and overreact to something before having all the facts. Asking more questions to gain a better understanding of the other person's intention is necessary - to ensure that your response is communicated effectively and appropriately.

9. **Be where you are and give it your full attention.**

Be in the present, focusing your awareness and giving your full attention to the activity that you are currently engaged in increases your opportunity for success and decreases levels of stress. In this case, stress is caused by being in one place wishing that you were in another.

10. **Know that you are equal; you are not less than or better than anyone else.**

Being treated without equality and being unequal are two very different ideas. All people are created equal with inherent rights to life, liberty and the pursuit of happiness. Each person contributes to society in their own way whether they are the president of an organization or they are the homeless.

11. Define your goals; know where you are going so that you know when you get there.

Having goals and objectives helps people with the planning process and allows them to monitor their progress over time. Otherwise, you remain in the same place unmotivated and not moving forward, never realizing your potential, accomplishments and successes.

12. Focus on the process and not on the outcome.

While having a desired outcome in mind is essential, you need to focus on your present activity. Focusing moment to moment or activity to activity will move you closer to your end result and increase your chance for overall success. That is to say, focus on each golf swing and not on the score! In this way, you give everything your best effort, increase your confidence and leave the outcome open for even greater possibility – still moving in your chosen direction.

13. Experience your life and enjoy all that it has to offer.

The best way to experience joy in your life is to make conscious choices coupled with practical everyday changes, have appreciation for the people in your life and do the things that you are best at.

14. Identify and understand all things that energize you.

People who are energizing: engage others by focusing on the possibilities rather than the limitations; are open to other people's points of view; speak their mind while maintaining integrity between their words and their actions; and maintain eye contact and give their undivided attention. There are many other things that energize people. Make a list, know what they are, be prepared.

15. Remove yourself from things, places and people that make you feel bad.

De-energizing behaviour from others can come across as criticizing or micromanaging - a put down. These people deplete others energy in their haste to find a solution, demonstrate their knowledge or force others to come around to their way of thinking. When there is a disagreement, they tend to focus on the individual rather than the issue at hand.

16. Place your attention on what is important.

Whatever you place your attention on in any area of our life, relationship or career, it will become stronger, healthier and successful. Attention requires operating in the present. Every action needs undivided attention to be fruitful.

17. Be strong and go courageously in the direction of your fears.

Leaping into a new possibility, rather than avoiding it, may be frightening. However, it also represents the best opportunities for growth. Say yes and figure it out as you go. It is okay to jump in a little over your head that is how you will learn. If you do not do things because you are afraid, you may never know what could have been. You may never reach your full potential, your best self, self-actualization.

18. Let your subconscious mind show you the way.

The subconscious mind stores your previous life experiences, your beliefs, your memories, your skills, all situations you have been through and the images that you have seen that the conscious mind may not immediately remember or process with full understanding.

It permanently stores everything that has happened to you for later retrieval. Your conscious mind can give your subconscious mind a command or a problem to solve, processing the data for you – consistent with your current programming.

19. Do not give up; be patient, positive and persevere.

Things don't always go as planned; people have good days and bad days. There will always be things that you cannot control. Managing setbacks and challenges effectively - seeing the light at the end of the tunnel - requires one to remain positive and patient, to persevere and not give up. When you fall get up, begin again and keep going.

20. Do not settle for good when you can have great.

Many people simply accept what happens to them or they go along with others choices and decisions making themselves feel unsettled and never quite happy with the end result. It is better to get the best that you can afford or go for the most that you can manage. Do not waste your time regretting what could have been or should have been. Spend your time and money wisely.

21. Know that you can rewrite your script at any time.

It is rarely too late to become who you always wanted to be. Rewriting your script, simply means, reassessing your strengths and preferences, putting them to work for you in a new way, exploring new possibilities and recognizing the experience that you already have.

22. Recognize your friends and nurture those relationships.

People are sometimes meant to come and go in our lives but friends are long-term and grow with us as our lives change. Friends energize each other with honesty and integrity.

23. Remain focused on your dreams.

Dreams can become a reality when you define your aspiration, eliminate unnecessary distractions and work on what is important to you.

24. Believe in yourself and it will happen.

Proceeding from the perspective of the solution, rather than the problem, helps you to be confident in yourself, places attention on the present, removes self-doubt, opens up new possibilities and places you in control of your result.

25. Know that everyone has their own unique story and perspective.

The way of regarding situations, facts or relative importance is based on life experience, beliefs and values. Therefore, anyone's opinion is neither right nor wrong. It is simply an opinion based on what they know, or in some cases, what they do not know.

26. Make your choices absolutely then your choices are easy.

If it is not an absolute yes then the answer is no. Sometimes there is no question about it; one knows what to do. However, there are many times that one hesitates, bouncing back and forth not sure which way to go. When the choice or decision is unclear, do not do it.

27. Pay attention to your instinct and do not dismiss it.

Your instinct, gut feeling or personal radar is built up over the years and plays an important role in the decision making process. In business, data or insight can be used to confirm your instinct if and when required. However, you cannot rely on your instinct when emotions are involved. Emotions blind your instincts – your common sense.

28. Recognize co-incidence; it is a sign post pointing you in the right direction.

A coincidence is an event or incident which, although is not deliberate, appears to have been planned or appears as if it is connected. When a coincidence arises, ask yourself, what is the significance or message here and pay attention – you may arrive at a sudden insight.

29. Make your own luck; success is achieved when preparation meets opportunity.

Some say that luck, success or failure, is brought on by chance rather than by one's own actions. However, if we fail to prepare, we prepare to fail and luck has little to do with it. Do not put off until tomorrow what you can do today. Stay on top of things, be prepared, opportunity is everywhere, don't miss out.

30. Do not be influenced by the negative opinions of others.

You should not believe everything you are told. People base their opinions on their own life programming and usually do not have all the facts. Listen to the voice inside of you.

31. Be mindful of what you see in others; it may be a reflection of yourself.

The traits that we see most clearly in others are the ones that are the strongest in ourselves. When we have a strong negative reaction to someone, we can be certain that they are reflecting traits that we also possess but have been unwilling to recognize – transformational roadblocks. We cannot change what we are not willing to acknowledge.

32. Do not confuse impact with intent.

People say and do things that can have a negative impact on us even when it was not their intention to do so. Therefore, they need to be responsible for their impact regardless of their intentions. It is also our responsibility to understand others intentions before we react or overreact. Likewise, we need to be fully aware of our own intentions - are they honourable - before we say or do anything.

33. Be willing to listen and continue to learn.

Be open-minded. A willingness to listen and to learn is an essential aspect of wisdom. Part of being willing to learn is about actively or emphatically listening. Emphatic listening is about giving someone your undivided attention without interrupting them. Consider making notes while you are listening to the other person so that you can make your point after that other person has finished.

34. Ask but do not demand.

You can ask for nearly anything from anyone when your request is genuine. Help others to understand what you are asking for or why you need something. Being genuine is not so much about what you are doing as it is about why you are doing it. Demanding and barking orders may work if you are trying to get people out of a burning building, otherwise, demands are met with resistance and no support. People will disengage and not care.

35. Consider only your own personal observations.

Idle talk and rumors, especially about the personal or private affairs of others, is unacceptable behaviour. Only make judgments based on what you have personally observed and not on gossip.

36. Do not try to change others; rather try and change yourself.

If you change how you feel then you will change how you think. If you change how you think then you will change what actions you take. When you change what actions you take, the responses you get will change too. With new responses come new outcomes.

37. Know and understand yourself and your path will be clear.

Self-mastery understands one's own emotional reactions, behaviours, habits, motivations and thought processes. Understanding oneself begins with self-reflection. To know your true - significant - self is beyond any labels based on what you do or what you have.

38. Understand others thoughts and feelings and see outside your own view of the world.

Empathy or perspective helps you understand or feel what another person is experiencing, from within their frame of reference, to put yourself in another person's shoes. While you can empathize with where others are at, it does not mean that you have to agree with them or become a follower.

39. Change what you can, accept what you cannot change, and leave what you cannot accept.

Sometimes changing what you can refers to you and not them. However, if things are beyond your control then you are left with two choices: accept things as they are or move on. When you are able to come face to face with reality and you make a conscious choice, no matter what your choice, you will move forward. Keep in mind that practicing gratitude and appreciation can turn denial into acceptance.

40. Embrace change, without it there is little growth.

Change keeps you moving forward rather than being stuck. Without change you live in the past missing the experiences of the present and preventing yourself from living the life you were meant to live.

41. Take small steps and make a big difference.

A year from now you may have wished that you had started today. You are never too young, too old, too bad, too good, too healthy, too sick, too thin, too fat, too rich or too poor to start again. If you do not take a step nothing changes. Your journey begins with the first small step. It does not matter how slowly you go as long as you do not stop.

42. Positively influence your own experience and destiny.

You have the power in the present moment to respond and be progressive or react and remain blocked. When you can keep your desired outcome in mind, as you make choices, you can influence your destiny. If you do not, you are likely to end up where you are heading.

43. Know that your greatest strength will come from your greatest hurt.

While it is impossible in the present moment to understand what good could come from your deepest hurts, with time, your strengths will be revealed. It is through the "battles you fight" that you will be inspired to some greater purpose and meaning. Then, whether you take action, or not, remains your choice.

44. Find a meaningful coach and mentor.

Coaches help you identify and focus on what is important, which in turn, accelerates progress and success. You hire a life or an executive coach for the same reason that world class athletes use coaches – it helps you meet personal and professional objectives.

45. Be an insatiable reader.

Reading – continuous learning · increases your understanding and knowledge of all things. And, while reading is also important to reduce stress, it also gives you a higher level of vocabulary and improves your imagination, memory and focus.

46. Experience other cultures.

Opening your mind to diversity and new perspective builds awareness and tolerance, not only of your own world but of the world at large. Travel the world. Embrace people's sameness and appreciate people's differences.

47. Change your focus from blame to contribution.

Most people blame others for everything. It is never their fault and thus conflict ensues. Always reflect on how you may have contributed to the end result, the circumstance that you find yourself in or the relationship that you are currently experiencing with others. Communicate what you could do differently and experience a different outcome.

48. Treat others how they wish to be treated.

It takes some effort to get to know friends, employees or colleagues and their preferences for attention or quiet accolades. Make the time. The rewards are worth it: commitment, engagement, loyalty.

49. Express your feelings with the right person, at the right time, and for the right reason.

Beware of the "water cooler" syndrome, the gathering place to talk about someone else to other people. Some people tell others about their problems or conflicts hoping to gain their sympathy and gain support and followers. It is better for you, and for them, if you redirect them to the right person.

50. Search for solutions.

You need to express yourself clearly to make sure that you are understood, gather enough information by asking powerful questions and listen intently so that you understand others situations. You must ensure that you are not responding to the wrong intention thus giving others the impression that you do not care.

51. Give it your all.

When you put forth your best effort consistently and passionately, no matter what the job, circumstance or project, you will be successful.

52. Share your talent and experience with the world.

It is your profound obligation to share your talent and experience with others, and in so doing, transform your world and the world beyond.

WHO WE BECOME

The Summons

One of the longer term working commitments I agreed to was with the Catholic Archdiocese. I made a two year promise to work on "The Summons" - an adult faith formation - and have since committed to a second two year term. My role as one of the Directors was to provide a personal growth component; the other Directors provided components on liturgy, theology, scripture & spirituality.

I was not expecting the vast impact that it would have on me personally.

I initially agreed to work with The Summons for other reasons, a request from a former colleague, and dear friend, who is now a Catholic Priest and to help participants on their own self-discovery journey. However, to my great surprise and humility, my own faith grew and it was I who took the quantum leap.

The essence of spirituality is the search to know our real self, to discover the true nature of consciousness. [109]

We must be open to a world of possibility because anything and everything is possible.

---

[109] Peter Russell

The Gift of Insight

Once the first term with The Summons had come to an end, each participant was asked to draw a name and speak about the person that they had come to know over the previous two years - honouring God's presence. The feedback I received, not only touched my heart, but gave me a new sense of self. What a wonderful gift, to receive this personal insight and be recharged!

"It is somehow difficult to begin this without it feeling like an introduction – but we all know Brenda and we have all witnessed who she is, how she has grown and most of all been touched by her presence.

Brenda's purpose here was to help us grow and discover ourselves – to live more truly from the unique creations we are. Clearly she has led by example. In the beginning we were presented with very professional, polished program – developed from experience with reflection and true wisdom. Brenda did not stop there though – over the two years she shared with us her own continuing journey including her concern and love for her family. It is so much easier to just tell people what they ought to do but she lives it and does so with humility and transparency. In the last few months especially her sharing made her not just a teacher or facilitator but a peer we could relate to. She has been a leader within the journey.

One of Brenda's greatest gifts is her sense of humor. Not because it is entertaining but because it brings with it a freedom and lightness. Those who have this gift change a room just by stepping into it – humor is the expression of something different though, something that needs no words. Even though Brenda is outspoken; it is not just her words that speak her presence. When people such as Brenda enter a room – somehow whether we see or hear them or not, we all breathe a sigh of relief and the atmosphere changes. Not just of the room but within ourselves.

I would like to share a quote by Henri Nouwen from his book "Bread for the Journey" that to me so truly describes Brenda and who she is to us!

"When you are interiorly free you call others to freedom, whether you know it or not. Freedom attracts wherever it appears. A free man or a free woman creates space where others feel safe and want to dwell. Our world is so full of conditions, demands, requirements and obligations that we often wonder what is expected of us. But when we meet a truly free person, there are no expectations, only an invitation to reach into ourselves and discover there our own freedom. Where true inner freedom is, there is God. And where God is, there we want to be"

Thank you for sharing - not just your knowledge with us - but your freedom and the presence of God within you." [110]

Spiritual Intervention

I am no stranger to religion. I have been baptized and confirmed, been a Sunday School Teacher and even a member of the Church Choir – can you imagine! I was raised to know right from wrong, say my prayers, bless the meal and be thankful; trusting that this kind of life was not only expected but typical.

"Religion is for people who are afraid of going to hell; spirituality is for those who have already been there." [111]

While this quote has an amusing perspective, I do agree that we need spirituality to successfully navigate life's journey.

---

[110] Summons Participant
[111] The Spirituality of Imperfection, Ernest Kurtz, Katherine Ketchum

It would be impossible for me to have a successful and meaningful life without the intervention of a higher power. And yes, I feel that I have already been there – hell that is!

While I am in constant communication, my method of prayer of late is more along the lines of a meditation of the heart. That is to say, I am more focused on the idea that all possibilities are awaiting my choice. For example, I choose to feel the joy in this day, I choose to have the inner strength to say no and I choose to mind only my own business. Or, I could say I am joy, I am steadfast, and I am compassion and so on!

However, like so many other areas of our lives, we gain greater understanding and perspective when we immerse ourselves and dig deeper - expanding our perspective and strengthening our knowledge. The Summons has certainly been instrumental for me, from a spiritual standpoint, not only because I needed to dig deeper in preparation for teaching the participants, but in creating a hunger to learn and gain greater personal spiritual insight.

"We seek help for what we cannot face or accomplish alone; in seeking help, we accept and admit our own powerlessness. And in that acceptance and admission, in the acknowledgement that we are not in control, spirituality is born."[112]

Spirituality embraces self-discovery because it helps us find relief from the pain we are experiencing. Helping us to understand what is wrong; we can begin to accept the reality! By accepting the reality, we wake up. When we wake up, we are able to take action. Taking action requires strength. Faith gives us the strength to follow through.

The road to peace begins with faith. [113]

---

[112] Ernest Kurtz and Katherine Ketcham
[113] 2 Peter1

While my work continues to focus on emotions and behaviours and their subsequent impact, we need to understand that we are not always in control and that we do not have all of the answers, consequently, honourable leadership goes way beyond a traditional set of established skills and abilities.

Active Compassion

Compassion is our response to the suffering of others and motivates us to help. Studies have suggested that while compassion is vital to a healthy mind, it also helps us to feel what others are feeling – to be empathetic. And, the action of a compassionate person creates a better sense of well-being for others and helps to reduce one's own stress. As research at Harvard University tells us that our first instinctive impulse is to help others, then it would appear that we are doing ourselves a great deal of good at the same time.

A compassionate person is one that accepts people for who they are and does not judge them. They appreciate how others may be feeling in challenging situations and give others their undivided attention – listening with empathy. They are not angry or aggressive, at home or at work.

"There is nobility in compassion, a beauty in empathy and a grace in forgiveness." [114]

We are becoming more aware of the good results that come from compassion and a life of meaning and purpose, which is quite the opposite of selfishness. By directing consistent attention and effort to our words and behaviours, we can reflect compassion in everything that we do, and create new habits!

---

[114] John Connolly

Practicing Mindfulness

The idea of living in the present moment is the most fundamental truth. Practicing mindfulness - living in the present moment - improves our mental and physical health. Mindfulness requires us to focus, and accept our thoughts and feelings, without judgment or negative self-talk. It is a practice of meditation and prayer that helps give our minds a break, moving our thoughts away from our difficulties toward an appreciation of what is most important to us.

"Realize deeply that the present moment is all you ever have. Make the now the primary focus of your life." [115]

Practicing mindfulness helps us to release our worries about the future and our regrets from the past. Some psychology experts believe that mindfulness works, in part, by helping people to accept their experiences – including painful emotions – rather than react to them with denial and blame.

When we can reach a place within ourselves where we are able to accept our reality without hesitation, we reach a state of grace. And in that moment, we leap forward. When I accepted the reality of being a single parent, I met my husband. When I accepted the reality of leaving the corporate world, I started my own business. In this way, each day, as we are able to fully accept what is - this doesn't mean to say that we accept that it is meant to be - we accelerate our journey, no longer stuck in any one place.

And, scientists have discovered that the benefits of mindfulness can help to relieve stress and improve sleep. It is also important in the treatment of depression, substance abuse and eating disorders. [116] And, they are currently examining mindfulness as a key element to happiness.

---

[115] Eckhart Tolle
[116] Adapted from Harvard Health Publications

Brenda Oliver

Knowledge, Science and Spirituality

The fact is that we have been sharing knowledge, experience and stories with those that follow since there were people to do so. And, those that came before us had the knowledge that we were all directly related to everything around us.

It was only a little more than twenty years ago that science substantiated that we - indeed - are all connected. Thus, explaining how our emotions and behaviours were affecting our health and well-being, the impact that we were having on others and them on us, and the emergence of emotional intelligence.

Scientist, Gregg Braden, and Author of the Lost Language of God, enlightens us on the scientific events.

In brief, quantum biologists, conducting DNA experiments in the 1990`s, discovered and validated the existence of a field of energy previously not recognized by science. This field of energy has no impact on time and distance and is referred to as non-local energy. Apparently, this is energy that already exists and that is everywhere all of the time. Science refers to this field of non-local energy as "the stuff that lives between the nothing - a tightly woven intelligent web that links all of creation," suggesting, that all of humanity is related through this energy force.

"This field of energy that Western Science discovered sounds very similar to the creative force described by our ancestors throughout ancient traditions. It sounds like the presence of God." [117]

Scientists refer to this web of energy as the Quantum Hologram - a powerful consciousness, an intelligent mind, a matrix, the mind of God. From a scientific perspective, the

---

[117] Gregg Baden, Scientist

language of Quantum Physics is viewed as the bridge to this consciousness. Furthermore, from the perspective of this Quantum Hologram, simply stated, they tell us that there are no them and us. We are all holographic – reflecting back on ourselves.

This would suggest that we take a long reflective observation in the mirror before we criticize the behaviour of others. Furthermore, it would suggest that if we are all one and the same, when you hurt me, you hurt the people connected to me, and vice versa. And it stands to reason that if people are hurting others, they are also hurting themselves in the process!

These DNA experiments also tell us that when stress, anger, hatred and jealousy are introduced into the DNA experiment, the DNA strand tightens and knots up. However, when gratitude, appreciation, love and compassion are introduced, the DNA strand relaxes and untwines allowing immune systems to function better.

This tells us that our emotions, and subsequent behaviour, have a direct and immediate impact on our health and well-being. Of-course, our health and well-being has an impact on our personal effectiveness, performance, productivity and engagement! This also helps us to understand why we do not feel well when we are living, or working, in destructive environments. And, it also explains why it is so important for those suffering from any disease to be surrounded by love, gratitude, appreciation and compassion. It allows their immune systems to function better.

Furthermore, the untwining of the DNA explains why these human emotions can reverse the physiological changes and damage caused by stress, both in the moment and long term. However, the reverse is also true. When the immune system is not functioning at full capacity, the knotting up of the DNA explains why we are always run down, fighting a cold and feeling exhausted.

As a result, scientists suggest, if this energy force has an intelligence that responds to human emotion, exists everywhere, is always present and is mirrored back to us as our life experience, then, we can conclude that we are participating in the events of our own lives.

And, as participants in our own lives are we then connected to this consciousness when we are living in the present moment, when we are mindful? Moreover, does it then stand to reason that if we are not living in the present moment, we become unplugged and disconnected?

"Thinking is only a small aspect of consciousness. Thought cannot exist without consciousness, but consciousness does not need thought." [118]

Science tells us that the entire universe is made up of pure energy. And pure energy is made up of vibration and frequency: frequency is the pattern flashing on and off and vibration is how fast energy contracts and expands.

"Gratitude, appreciation, thankfulness can shift your energy, raise your vibration, and make all your next moments even better." [119]

Deepak Chopra implies that the more enlightened we become as human beings, the higher our frequency.

Are we on the same wavelength yet?

As human beings, we too are full of energy – we come fully charged. In fact, each of our 50 trillion cells has 1.7 volts of electrical power and these cells are constantly storing and

---

[118] Eckhart Tolle
[119] Joe Vitale

releasing energy. No wonder, we are endlessly searching to be reenergized and why we feel so weary when we are around difficult people and destructive environments. Their behaviours are draining us! And of-course, there is the whole myriad of physiological changes that occur making us weak and depleted.

Additionally in 2002, scientist John Wheeler suggested, when we actually look for something, this field of consciousness begins to build what we are looking for. While this suggests that we can influence our desired outcome, "believe it and you can achieve it", we also need to be cognizant that our thoughts – negative or positive - are influencing our day to day lives. While this "building what we are looking for" supports the power of prayer and meditation - be careful what you wish for!

Finally, scientists are talking about something called Super String Theory, suggesting that our world is made of different dimensions. Proposing that there are many possibilities that already exist and we are choosing a particular life experience based on our choices. They also suggest that we can leap from possibility to possibility, subsequently, changing the end result.

Great news! This means just because we have started down one path does not mean to say that we have to remain there. We can change our path at any time and thereby experience a different outcome, based on our own aspiration. We can make the quantum leap, from one path to another, of our choosing. However, this also suggests that an "unconscious" choice could position us on a path of destruction.

However, while there may be a pre-ordained plan for each of our lives, consider this. If we can live in the present moment, we will be in a positive state of mind. This state of mind will allow us to remain connected, give us the ability to make informed choices and decisions, and gain the internal strength to follow through. Ideally, making the journeys intended for us.

If we now understand that we are empowered to participate in the events of our own lives, we must also understand that our collective energy of emotions, thoughts and feelings are impacting us and those around us. Consequently, this suggests, when we can consciously change our thoughts, emotions and feelings, and the impact they have on us and others, we can influence our health, relationships and our lives.

"Insight on its own is an intellectual comfort. Power on its own is a blind force that can destroy as well as build. It is only when we link the two, insight and power that we sense not only our greatness and wisdom but also our capacity to allow this greatness to affect powerful change in others and ourselves." [120]

Each of us has been given the power to preserve or destroy. Daily, we make choices that influence our worlds and determine our end game. Will we be conscious and active participants in our own lives, and in so doing, change our worlds for the better?

"My freedom and independence do not depend on my acts of defiance or confrontation; they depend on my own attitudes and feelings. If I am always reacting, then I am never free." [121]

Let the challenge begin with me.

The Freedom Years

Working full time in my business included long term contracts, which changed my focus from online interaction to face to face business activities. And, while I continue in my Leadership

---

[120] Julia Cameron
[121] Al-Anon

Development Practice, we also enjoy golfing, leisure travel and a warmer climate in the winter months. While I remain busy, it is not work. I love what I do and cannot imagine being involved in anything else.

In life, as in business, there will always be challenges and setbacks. Those are unlikely to change but what I do about them surely has. And, while the road may, or may not, get easier; be assured, you will become stronger.

Also, despite the fact that our children may temporarily need our help, from time to time, and we may find some of our spare time filled with our grandchildren, rather than golf, we need only focus on today. And today is a great day.

Speaking of grandchildren, they are a valuable gift. Grandchildren give us the opportunity to experience the true nature of joy and happiness. We now have the time to understand the beauty and the miracle that we may have missed as young busy parents. They are a real blessing that completely erase all ravages of time, stress and anxiety – both past and present. They renew us!

"Let us be grateful to the people who make us happy; they are the gardeners who make our souls blossom." [122]

Have I any regrets? Did I make mistakes? Would I do anything differently given the opportunity? I certainly would have made different choices if I knew then what I know now. If I would not do anything differently, I would have to conclude that I had not learned anything from my life!

And there it is - the "ah ha" moment!

It is our utmost responsibility to share what we have learned, especially with those that follow, so they can benefit from our

---

[122] Marcel Proust

trials and tribulations. Perhaps even circumvent the damage along the way. Understanding, they can experience their own personal freedoms and any possibility of their choosing during their lifespan.

Sharing experiences, giving others a heads up on some of the problems that they could face and helping them to understand how to act and live in a variety of circumstances is wise and honourable.

And for those who are already wise, listen to your parents and become even wiser. Be the leaders - bringing honour to your own worlds. There is nothing to be gained by refusing to be taught. Wise men and women are happy to be instructed.

Can we continue to benefit from accumulated wisdom - the kind of wisdom that allows discussion, forgiveness and good deeds; the kind of wisdom that is passionate, straight forward and sincere?

We have a choice and with that choice, the power to preserve or destroy. The choices we make determine who we become. Who we become creates our future. With our transition comes renewal. With renewal comes freedom. With freedom comes positive influence. When we change, the worlds around us – friends, family and connections - are motivated to change in response. While some people consider that they have freedom when they can do whatever they want to do without restriction; the reality is that they only experience true freedom when they can stop doing those things!

"Freedom is not the right to do what we want, but what we ought. Let us have faith that right makes might and in that faith let us; to the end, dare to do our duty as we understand it." [123]

---

[123] Abraham Lincoln

Our journey to personal success begins with being the best that we can be; at whatever we do, with whom we choose to be with or with those we come in contact with. Giving these relationships, careers or activities our very best - our all. During this journey, we come to realize that there is a higher power, something bigger than ourselves.

Along the way, we discover our purpose. We reach a place and time when we are no longer ruled by our personality - our ego - and we leave selfishness behind. We move forward, not remaining stuck in any one place. We become patient. Our behaviours change and we become open to receiving direction. We experience personal growth.

We genuinely like and enjoy other people, loving all things passionately. We are renewed and reenergized. We experience spiritual growth. We become more effective. We are fully conscious, appreciative and thankful. We live with kindness - honouring progressive behaviours- being productive. We are at peace. The road to health, happiness and peace of mind does not have to take a lifetime!

"Real change will take place when individuals transform themselves, guided by the values that lie at the core of all human ethical systems, scientific findings, and common sense." [124]

Can individuals continue to benefit from the wisdom, knowledge and experience of others - learning from their challenges, successes and history?

"There is no passion to be found in playing small – settling for a life that is less than the one that you are capable of living." [125]

My long walk has not yet ended...

---

[124] Dali Lama
[125] Nelson Mandela

THE AUTHOR

Brenda Oliver, leadership & performance expert was born in Ontario, Canada. A finalist in the Business Woman Entrepreneur of the Year Awards, she is the owner and president of Oliver Leadership Inc. – a Leadership Development Practice since 2003 – giving clients the competitive advantage to transform their personal, professional and business performance, through custom keynotes, professional development workshops, executive & life coaching and business consulting services.

With more than 25 years of corporate experience in strategic business development, sales planning, individual coaching, training & development, relationship management, marketing, consulting services and a successful professional career that has included a variety of senior management and executive positions within the financial services and insurance industries – a former Director with American Express – Brenda Oliver is an Speaker, Coach, Consultant and Author offering both inspirational and business insight to a variety of groups and venues.

Her experience and enthusiasm enables individuals and organizations to capitalize on their human potential in the most effective manner. She has clearly demonstrated her ability to develop, inspire and lead people – helping others to succeed and reach their greatest potential.

As a Certified Practitioner in Emotional Intelligence & Performance Evaluation; she continues to work with executives and groups to facilitate and offer perspective, structured process & professional development.

As a published Author of her book, The Freedom Challenge, Mastering Emotions – Restoring Honour to Leadership and with published articles with Toastmasters International, the Human Resource Institute of Alberta and Evan Carmichael; she blends business experience and expertise with real life experience.

As a Professional Speaker with the Canadian Association of Professional Speakers (CAPS) and Global Speakers Association (GSF) she delivers her message on Leadership and Performance with passion, inspiration and humor; sharing her life experiences, career challenges and success stories.

As a Certified Executive & Life Mastery Coach; she ensures accountability, provides objective views, keeps participants focused, provides disciplined process, offers a sounding board and provides motivation to Individuals, Managers and Executive.

As a Strategic Consultant delivering Business Planning Process and Practices; she ensures the desired results/output on specific projects are achieved in a timely manner permitting management and executive to focus on the day to day requirements of the organization.

As a Corporate Trainer & Facilitator; she inspires innovation and learning, delivers foundational and practical tools that are hands-on & educational, enables workshops that engage and challenge participants and meets the needs of employees and leaders at different levels of the organization.

Oliver Leadership Inc. offers a full range of Corporate & Educational Training Materials & Custom Options - including Foundational Training in Emotional Intelligence Fundamentals, Communication Strategy and Developing Personal Goals - delivering learning and Professional Development Programs that enhance business training programs, professional development days, meetings and conferences that will be ideal for any organization.

All programs are interactive and experiential with power point presentations, including workbooks and handouts as required.

"Brenda Oliver employs a progressive, strategic system that is both practical and illuminating, with tools that are immediately effective as well as transferable to nearly every area of one's life. For those wanting to go a little more in depth, they get beneath the surface and offer some deeper insights and large opportunities for improvement and development. My experience is that Brenda Oliver provides immense value for the initiate and knowledgeable alike, supplying real tools not often observed elsewhere and creates an immediate, profound impact on both one's professional development as well as one's personal life." [126]

To receive weekly leadership messages visit, <u>www. BrendaOliver.com</u> and join the global network. Linked In <u>https://ca.linkedin.com/in/oliverleadership</u>

---

[126] A. James

Printed in the United States
By Bookmasters